THE OPENING ACT

COMEDY, LIFE AND THE
DESPERATE PURSUIT OF HAPPINESS

THE OPENING ACT

COMEDY, LIFE AND THE
DESPERATE PURSUIT OF HAPPINESS

Larry Noto
with Kevin Cowherd

Apprentice House
Loyola University Maryland
Baltimore, Maryland

First Edition

Printed in the United States of America

Hardcover ISBN: 978-1-62720-091-2
Paperback ISBN: 978-1-62720-092-9
E-book ISBN: 978-1-62720-093-6

Design: Apprentice House
Editorial Development: Alice Maule

Published by Apprentice House

Apprentice House
Loyola University Maryland
4501 N. Charles Street
Baltimore, MD 21210
410.617.5265 • 410.617.2198 (fax)
www.ApprenticeHouse.com
info@ApprenticeHouse.com

Dedicated to my mom and dad, who raised me to appreciate the joy in life.

A SPECIAL THANK YOU TO THESE OFFICIAL SUPPORTERS

Joe and Donna Noto

Amanda and Dustin Bentkowski
James and Juli Dempsey
Garth and Jennifer Gerhart
M Brent Trostle and Nancy Nuth
Lee Rose

Anne Mannix and Mark Brown
Wayne Buder
Maria Gruzynski
Amanda and Patrick Preller
Marni Sacks
Essam Shomali
Mary-Margaret Stepanian
Andrew Unger

Josephine and Bernie Batzer

Bob and Pam DelVerne

Amy Elias

Kevin Hoppe

Helen Krammar

Yelee Kim

Laura Lang

Tim and Beth Lavery

Tracey Harrington McCoy

Pammy and Junior Miller

Michele Petti

Sam Puleo

Sean Somerville

Howard and Sandy Schapiro

Sergio Vitale

Ray and Joanne Weiss

Special thanks to our additional Kickstarter supporters, Aldo's Ristorante Italiano, Kevin Atticks, comedian Mike Finazzo, designer Garth Gerhart, Alice Maule, Magooby's Joke House, and to the friendly staff at the Nautilus Diner in Timonium, where we spent many evenings over many meals putting the book together.

CONTENTS

Introduction.. 1

Larry Live: How About This Weather? 5

Chapter 1: Early Expectations 9

Larry Live: Birthdays 16

Chapter 2: Innocence Drop-Kicked 19

Larry Live: The Airport.. 24

Chapter 3: "The Larry Noto Show" 27

Larry Live: Snow Globes.. 35

Chapter 4: A Small Taste of the Big Time.................... 39

Larry Live: Passion of the Christ 45

Chapter 5: Charming 'Em in Charm City..................... 47

Larry Live: Italian Nicknames.................................... 53

Chapter 6: The Opportunity of a Lifetime 55

Larry Live: The Bus Ad.. 60

Chapter 7: The Great Dom Irrera................................ 63

Larry Live: The Wedding Shower............................... 67

Chapter 8: Driving Richard Lewis................................ 69

Larry Live: Speed Dating... 75

Chapter 9: Learning at the Feet of the Masters 77

Larry Live: Being Catholic... 82

And Now: An Album 85

Chapter 10: "I'm Gonna Help You Out" 113

Larry Live: Random Thoughts 118

Chapter 11: "The Night the Laughter Died" 121

Larry Live: Wild World of Sports 127

Chapter 12: The Great Escape 129

Larry Live: Dating 133

Chapter 13: Meet the Neighbors 135

Larry Live: Law & Order 139

Chapter 14: Picking Up the Pieces 141

Larry Live: More Random Thoughts 145

Chapter 15: "Oh, You Think You're a Comedian?" 149

Larry Live: The Gym 155

Chapter 16: Rolling the Dice – and Finally a Payoff 157

Larry Live: Burger King 166

Chapter 17: Behind the Scenes: It Can Get Ugly 169

Larry Live: Target 174

Chapter 18: I Got This Idea 177

Larry Live: "Wheel of Fortune" 189

Chapter 19: A Night to Remember 193

Epilogue 199

About the Authors 203

"Life is made up of a few big moments, and a lot of little ones. I still remember the first time I kissed Sylvia . . . And I still remember that white-bread sandwich and that blonde dancing girl with the cigarette pack on her thigh. But a lot of images fade, and no matter how hard I try, I can't get them back. I had a relative once who said that 'If I knew things would no longer be, I would have tried to remember better.'"

—Ben Kurtzman in Barry Levinson's "Liberty Heights"

"I believe that if, at the end, according to our abilities, we have done something to make others a little happier, and something to make ourselves a little happier, that is about the best we can do. To make others less happy is a crime. To make ourselves unhappy is where all crime starts. We must try to contribute joy to the world. That is true no matter what our problems, our health, our circumstances. We must try. I didn't always know this, but am happy I lived long enough to find out."

—Roger Ebert, from "Life Itself."

INTRODUCTION

It's 2 a.m. on a warm July night in 2003 and I'm having dinner at Sabatino's in Baltimore's Little Italy, a neighborhood I've been coming to since I was a kid.

I've had graduation dinners here. Rehearsal dinners. First dates. Last dates. Only dates.

But tonight is different.

Tonight I'm having dinner with Dom Irrera.

Dom Irrera: named one of the top 100 comedians of all time.

Dom Irrera: the comic I loved watching on HBO and Comedy Central.

Dom Irrera: the funnyman with the sad, basset hound eyes who starred in a great episode of "Seinfeld."

Tonight it's Dom and me.

And not because I won some fan contest. Or because I'm some kind of nut job celebrity stalker.

It's because I'm a paid comedian now. Sure, I'm still young. But I was Dom Irrera's opening act the past four nights, after which he said: "Hey, want to grab something to eat?"

(What was I going to say to one of my comedy idols? "Hey, Dom, I'm a little busy, OK? Now quit bugging me?")

Still, as we savor our gnocchi and chat about the business, I'm amazed at my good fortune.

See, in some ways, I'm still the kid from Harford County who wasn't allowed to drive I-95 because my parents thought it was like driving the Indy 500.

I'm still the kid who lived at home until he was 30, because when you're the son of Italian immigrants, prison is easier to break out of than your parents' house.

I'm still the kid who dreamed of being a comedian and being on TV as far back as I can remember. (In the womb, I probably tapped the umbilical cord and said: "Is this thing on?")

As we wrap up dinner, Dom is recognized by a group at a nearby table. They gesture for us to come over.

One guy says: "Hey, you're Dom Irrera! We love you!" Then they turn to me. I'm standing behind Dom, off to one side. "And you're the kid who opened for him!"

Unbelievable!

I've been recognized in a restaurant! By the public! Immediately I start scanning the walls for a place where they can hang my auto-graphed headshot, which management will surely ask for now.

Dom looks at me and, smiling, says: "Oh, God, this'll go to his head."

Because he *knows*. He knows I have something inside of me that's needed to come out for years. Something about being a comedian . . . being on stage . . . being recognized.

Being a star.

This moment with Dom is the icing on the cake on what's been one of the coolest weekends of my life. I'm getting paid to perform at the top comedy club in Baltimore, the Improv, the most-recognizable brand in the business. I just opened for one of comedy's true originals.

And while I'm happy, I'm also filled with . . . an underlying cur-rent of anxiety.

Because I know these are my final moments with Dom this week-end. In just a few moments, he'll climb into a cab, go back to his hotel and fly to Los Angeles in the morning.

And me . . . I'll still be here. In Baltimore. Sure, it's a town I love. But it's not exactly a comedy Mecca.

Will I get to talk to Dom again? Will I get to work with him again? Will I even get booked at the Improv again? All of this is up in the air.

As we leave Sabs, Dom says: "OK, guess I'll see you next time I'm in town."

I want to jump in his arms and beg him to take me with him. Take me on the road, Dom! Let me open for you all the time! Tell your agent about me! Help the world discover me, Dom! *PLEASE!*

But I keep it all inside. I don't want to ruin the purity of the moment.

Dom gets in the cab and it slowly drives away.

He's going. I'm staying. And that sums it all up.

Now flash forward to the present. All these years later, I'm still the opening act.

But you're wasting your tears if you cry for me, folks. I've been fortunate in so many ways. I've opened for comedy legends like Richard Lewis, Paul Reiser, Brad Garrett, Lewis Black, Louie Anderson, Bob Saget, Brian Regan and Damon Wayans.

I've performed in New York and Las Vegas. I've been on TV and radio.

I've done corporate gigs in front of 2,500 people – you haven't lived until you've worked the American Bus Association convention and had tour operators spitting your lines back at you an hour later, like you're the funniest guy in the world.

But the truth is, even though I always wanted to be a big star, I never really went for it. Never moved to Manhattan or L.A., never played every crappy open-mic night and soul-sucking 1 a.m. gig in front of 50 drunks until I was – God, I hate this word – *discovered.*

And that's really what this book is all about.

It's about having a dream and getting a taste of it, but also knowing you weren't willing to risk it all in order to make it.

It's about finding happiness in what you've accomplished versus dwelling on what you haven't – or envying others for what they have.

It's about discovering a life purpose and defining success based on that – and not the judgment or perception of others.

These days, after a seismic change in my life – more on this later – my day job is running the music store my dad founded and nurtured up until his death last May.

What else can I tell you about myself?

I'm 39, though I look – he said modestly – 38. I have no kids of my own but my friends have more than Brad and Angelina, so I'm "Uncle Larry" to a small village. I own my own Muppets, go to Walt Disney World at least once a year and I put up over a dozen Christmas trees in my home each year. Somehow, though, I still manage to attract women.

My neighbor is a nun *and* a psychoanalyst and I have a mild obsession with Target (which the nun and I are working through . . . but that's for another book.)

Any or all of the above would give a comic enough material for 100 years. But I only do about a dozen stand-up gigs a year now.

And guess what? I'm finally at peace with that. It took a long time for me to feel that way, but I do.

This is my story.

LARRY LIVE

How About This Weather?

I'm not sure what's going on with Mother Nature. I'm not sure if she's drunk or high or PMS-ing. But she's clearly pissed off.

We even had an earthquake here a few years ago! On the East Coast! In Baltimore!

OK, fine, it was a minor earthquake. But you would have thought it was the Big One hitting. It just proved that we as a town could never handle an actual earthquake.

Have you seen news reports of the earthquakes out west? The earth opens! Cars disappear! Buildings collapse!

Our news reports were a little less dramatic . . .

TUNE IN TONIGHT AT 11 TO SEE THE INCREDIBLE FOOTAGE OF CUPS AND SAUCERS FALLING OFF A SHELF!

BREAKING NEWS! A WOMAN LOST A HUMMEL!

And the people in Baltimore had clearly lost their minds. "Oh, my God, it was one of the scariest things we've ever been through! When I got home from work, three or four pictures were crooked!

So we're not used to earthquakes. But we SHOULD be used to snow and cold weather by now. And yet it happens every year: round-the-clock news coverage. We don't go to work. Kids don't go to school.

We board up the houses and send everyone to Mexico.

You know those survivalists who prepare for the Apocalypse? They have NOTHING on people in this town getting ready for a snowstorm.

People hate to get snowed in. It's a concept I don't understand. I LOVE to be snowed in. Are you kidding me? It's like a hall pass from Mother Nature. Like someone saying: "Hey, you! You don't have to go out and do anything!"

Half my life, I wish I was snowed in . . .

Like when I'm in the movie theater with some asshole talking and kicking the back of my seat . . . who wouldn't want to be snowed in?

But I live in a court of shoveling Nazis. As soon as the first snowflake falls, they're out there shoveling. Morning, noon and night they're shoveling. Down to the pavement. Hell, down to the lawn!

They're out there at 2 a.m. with flood lamps, a leaf blower and a mule moving snow. The Chilean miners didn't try this hard to get out! I'm in my house in my pajamas trying to enjoy some coffee and the rare opportunity to watch "The Price is Right" – and my neighbor is out there with a hair dryer tunneling his way to the highway.

He's actually out there right now shoveling. Oh wait, he did my sidewalk and steps . . . good guy.

We don't even have normal storms anymore. Now we have storms that hit so hard and fast that people literally leave their cars on the highway. THEY WALK AWAY FROM THEIR CARS! IN THE MIDDLE OF A STORM!

"Yeah, I know we paid $40,000 for this car, honey. But we need to move on . . ."

We had a snowstorm where it started to thunder. Yes! Thunder! And people lost their fucking minds!

The weather people started to call it Thunder Snow. They didn't know what else to call it! The news stations scrambled 'cause they didn't know what cute little symbol to put in the corner of the screen. It was like, "We don't have a symbol for Thunder Snow! What graphic do I put up?!"

I don't know . . . how about a question mark and a middle finger?

It would get your attention though, wouldn't it? If you were at home watching "The Wheel of Fortune" and all of a sudden a middle finger appeared in the bottom of your screen?

"Honey . . . Where are the flashlights? I think something bad is coming . . ."

Thunder Snow. Sounds like a heavy metal band.

Thunder Snow. Sounds like a fat white stripper.

"Now coming to the stage . . . give it up for Thunder Snow!"

(Sigh.) I wish I was snowed in again already.

CHAPTER 1

EARLY EXPECTATIONS

Ever since I was a kid, people have told me: "We're going to see you on Letterman someday." Or: "You're going to be a comedian, we'll be seeing you on TV." From the very beginning, it was as if there was an intricate master plan in place for my career.

I grew up in Bel Air, Maryland, a suburb north of Baltimore, where the big news was the opening of an Old Navy at the mall.

My father, Joe, was born in Sicily, emigrated to the U.S. when he was 16 and eventually opened a music store. My mom, Donna, came from an Italian family with roots in Uniontown, Pa., an old coal-mining town an hour south of Pittsburgh.

If you're an NFL fan, you know this is deep in Steelers Country. But mercifully she grew up in Charm City and her and my grandparents made the righteous decision to root for the Colts. And after evil owner Robert Irsay whisked the team to Indianapolis in the dead of night as if it were nothing more than a box of Tupperware, she became a Ravens fan.

As a baby, I was full of energy and needed to be entertained constantly. When I cried, my folks had to literally do song-and-dance acts to get me to shut up. When I was older, my grandparents Tony and Juliet Sansone, would sing Sinatra tunes to me in the car. My grandfather and I would trade corny jokes. ("Doc, it hurts when I do this! Then don't do that!")

Think about it: I'm 6 years old and doing vaudeville!

Then there was my sister, Amanda, five years younger, who was blessed with the musical gene that largely bypassed me.

My sister and I would record funny videos to make our family laugh. And remember, in our day, we didn't have iMovie and YouTube. We were using VHS tapes and VCRs to pull off this state-of-the-art production! We'd do skits and characters we saw on "The Carol Burnett Show" and "Saturday Night Live."

I didn't know who Julia Child was, but I could do an impression of Dan Aykroyd doing an impression of Julia Child.

And people wonder where this deep-seated need to entertain comes from . . .

The house was always spotless. But my mom didn't put up with impromptu visits from anyone. My line was: I could have friends over – but with a month's written notice and a deposit for the painters and carpet cleaners.

There were no "drop-bys." If you dropped by, she dropped dead. (Bada-boom!)

The whole family was obsessed with pop culture – especially movies and sitcoms. You know that scene in "My Big Fat Greek Wedding" where Toula sits between her parents on the couch watching TV? That's like a documentary of my life.

My parents were strict. No smoking, no drinking, no partying. And definitely no cursing.

I remember begging my parents to let me watch "Police Academy." Finally my dad dubbed a tape and muted out the curse words by hand using the remote! Which was about 90 per cent of the audio. Imagine how horrible this was. To me, "Police Academy" was a silent film!

We all loved "Soap," the parody of soap operas that was such a big hit in the late '70s. My father taped every episode without commercial breaks. We would memorize entire scenes, and reciting lines to each other became a tradition and a part of almost any family dialogue.

Like the one where there's an explosion in the kitchen and Saunders, the butler, emerges from a cloud of smoke. Covered in soot, he announces in a lofty manner: "Mrs. Tate, when you're ready, dinner is on the stove. The stove, however, is in the pool."

If you wanted to make my mom howl, you trotted out lines from "Frasier," the early '90s sitcom starring Kelsey Grammer about the Boston therapist who moves to Seattle for a fresh start.

One of her personal favorites was Frasier's retort after hearing Daphne and Martin bicker for several minutes over exchanging gifts: "Good Lord, it's like Christmas morning in the Gambino household!"

But this was my life. Even at an early age, I'd watch comedians on TV and in the movies. I'd idolize them. Study them. Mimic them.

I'd learn their mannerisms. Their inflections. I didn't just remember lines from TV shows and movies – I remembered *exactly* how they were delivered and I'd repeat that delivery for friends and family in the exact same way.

It was more than doing impressions – it was a channeling of their inner comedian.

I honestly believe all this TV watching and family by-play helped make me funny. And luckily for me, my family raised me on a balanced diet of the greats – Mel Brooks, Peter Sellers, Johnny Carson, Norman Lear, Carl Reiner, Woody Allen.

My childhood slogan may well have been "Wit: It Does a Body Good."

The journey for me was to find my own voice and develop my own material, which started for real in high school.

I attended John Carroll, a nearby Catholic school, where two women were instrumental in pushing me toward the spotlight.

The first was a white-haired, stern-looking nun named Sister Marie Gregory. After I did one of the scripture readings at an assembly, she approached me during lunch one day.

"I'm the head of the Forensics Club," she said, "and I think you'd be a great at it."

I thanked her profusely and said I was very flattered. Then I went back to the lunch table and asked one of my friends: what the hell is forensics?

"That's where they examine dead bodies," he said.

And I thought: she thinks I'd be great at that?!

But in this case, forensics turned out to be a combination of public speaking, story telling, improvisation and dramatic interpretation. My main acting partner, Michelle Kanotz, and I competed with schools all around Baltimore, performing everything from the classic Abbott and Costello sketch "Who's on First?" to scenes from "Driving Miss Daisy" and "Butterflies Are Free." We won state championships and became the Sonny and Cher of the Maryland Forensics League – if Sonny and Cher were driven around by a nun in a giant station wagon.

A scene from "Brighton Beach Memoirs" got me to the nationals in Boca Raton, Fla. No one in my family had been on a plane since a mechanical issue caused a very close call on a flight we were on when I was 10. But as the saying goes, if you're going to fly . . . fly with a nun.

At the Maryland Scene Festival, an acting competition, I broke out the famous "You can't handle the truth!" speech from "A Few Good Men," when a snarling, defiant Col. Nathan R. Jessep (Jack Nicholson) fairly spits:

"Son, we live in a world that has walls, and those walls have to be guarded by men with guns. Who's gonna do it? You? *You*, Lt. Weinburg? I have a greater responsibility than you could possibly fathom . . ."

I must have done a good job channeling the unhinged Marine commanding officer, because I took first place and won a modest scholarship, too.

While acting was my passion, I also participated in some debates and ran track and cross-country. I could win an argument with someone. Or if not, outrun them.

The Senior Variety Show, an annual, much-anticipated extravaganza at John Carroll, was another milestone on my way to being an entertainer. It was the first time I wrote material for the stage. I wrote some 20 sketches as well as a big musical number riffing off Paul Simon's "You Can Call Me Al" that incorporated my classmates.

Standing back-stage and watching classmates recite lines that I wrote – and getting laughs! – was a surreal and wonderful experience.

The other woman at John Carroll who had such a profound impact on my early life was Laura Lang, who was the head of the alumni office and also directed school plays. She directed me in "Hello, Dolly!" and was always talking me up.

Years later, she would tell people that I was one of those kids in high school who just stood out. Of the students who participate in plays, she'd say, 50 per cent have no talent, 49.9 per cent have some modicum of talent and .001 have some special quality about them that could lead to, well, stardom.

For some reason (aw, there I go being humble again), she lumped me in that last group. She was also one of the first people to tell me I should do stand-up comedy.

"Go do some open-mic nights," she'd say. "They have one at Winchester's Comedy Club in Baltimore."

Great, I thought.

Uh, what's an open-mic night?

Besides not knowing what she was talking about, the fact that Winchester's was in Baltimore posed a major problem.

Since I wasn't allowed to drive to Baltimore – to listen to my parents, you'd have thought I was trying to get to Paris – I got my friend Janine DiPaula to drive me.

Here I was, 17 years old and barely a month out of high school, going to my first real gig. I was nervous and excited. The club was in a three-floor building on Water Street. The open-mic stuff was held in the downstairs bar, on a tiny stage with a stool, a microphone and bad lighting.

The crowd was – how to put this? – sparse. A few people doing stand-up for the first time. A few of their friends. One or two seasoned comics trying to work out new material. A couple of drunks. That was it.

I did maybe six minutes that night – and somehow survived. I didn't have any material. Hell, I wasn't a *real* comedian! So what I did was stuff I'd done with the Forensics Club. In this case, it was a piece from "Sure Thing." That's the comic play by David Ives about a conversation between two people that keeps starting over when one of them responds negatively to the other and a bell rings. (I used a buzzer from the Hasbro party game Taboo. Sue me.)

But I guess I wasn't terrible. Because afterward the manager said: "That was really funny. How old are you?"

I told him I'd be 18 soon. He was incredulous.

"What are you even *doing* here?!" he said.

Nevertheless, he booked me to do another gig a few weeks later for a bunch of young summer campers. I opened for Andre Brown, a veteran Baltimore comedian. This was on the top floor of Winchester's. I felt like I had moved up to the big room, to the Copa!

Looking back on it now, I'd be embarrassed to perform the stuff I performed back then. And the truth was, some of the jokes were ones I had probably read in some book. What can I say? I was young and desperate for material. That's how it is in the beginning.

I was also taking the first tentative steps to see where stand-up could lead me. So a month or so later, I was off to New York with Laura Lang to do an open-mic night at the New York Comedy Club.

It was first trip to Manhattan and I remember calling my mom from Times Square on a pay phone. (Kids, you can Google this phenomenon – a pay phone – on your iPhone.)

If you think visiting New York for the first time is daunting, imagine *playing* the Big Apple on the same trip! But I managed to control my nerves and do well. Laura said that as soon as I got the first laugh of my seven-minute set, you could see the transformation in my face.

It was like: *OK, this is what I was meant to do.*

I guess I impressed the club's manager, because after the show he asked: "What are you doing Wednesday?" He was putting a showcase together and invited me to appear.

But I politely declined, adding that I was just visiting the city. Hell, I wasn't allowed to drive to Baltimore! And I was gonna come back to New York on Wednesday?

Looking back on it now, that moment symbolized everything.

Here was a golden opportunity to play in the comedy capital of the world, where major talent was discovered all the time – for a club manager who liked me! And I didn't go for it.

I was in the wrong place. I was in Baltimore, not Manhattan.

Glittering opportunities like that don't come along every day. But I was too young to see that.

Maybe I wasn't ready to fully commit to comedy back then, either. My father and mother, after all, were realists. They were extremely supportive, but they wanted a safer path, a more secure future for me based on a good education. They wanted me to have a good life, and I'm blessed that they did.

The other thing was, my parents never understood the need to have strangers love and admire you. They hated the Hollywood scene and felt it was filled with ugly people and drugs, and that somehow I'd get chewed up by it.

I used to joke: they believed I was great enough to have the world know me. They just wanted the world to come to our basement. If it were up to them, I wouldn't play Los Angeles. I'd play our backyard – with plenty of advance notice, of course.

But I was never going to be satisfied with that.

I had much bigger plans.

LARRY LIVE

Birthdays

I have to be honest. I don't understand birthday celebrations.

You get cards, gifts, a cake . . . for what? The anniversary of your birth?

Something you had nothing to do with?

When you think about it, your MOM is the one who did all the work. I think you should buy HER a card.

I do like getting birthday cards from people I know. It's always nice.

Buying cards for someone, though, is basically a pain in the ass.

Have you ever tried to buy a card for someone and all the cards are like 100 times nicer than any ACTUAL sentiment you want to express to the person?

Ever pick up a card, read it, then put it back . . . 'cause it was TOO much love for the person?

Who are these people at Hallmark living these fairy-tale lives? Apparently they know much better people than we do.

I had to buy a card recently and every card was over-the-top.

"God blessed us when He put you on the earth."

No, he fucking didn't. Back on the shelf you go!

"Thanks for always being there for me."

Nope! Not even going to read the inside. We barely talk! I don't even know why I'm buying you a card, to be honest.

This is why I could never work for Hallmark. My cards would be more real. My cards would tell it like it is:

"You're a bitch to everyone around you. Shit rolls downhill. Thanks for ruining all our lives. Fuck you. Merry Christmas!"

And then it would play music . . .

I think some of you would actually buy that card if you could.

Now they have cards that let YOU record a special message.

I don't want this! I don't know what to say! THAT'S why I'm buying the card. I want YOU to say it for me!

I accidentally bought one, though, and was forced to record a message.

So I did . . .

"Hi . . . um . . . yeah... read the card."

When you care enough to send the very best . . .

CHAPTER 2

INNOCENCE DROP-KICKED

The summer after high school also marked my first brush with a stock character in the seamy netherworld of stand-up comedy: the smooth-talking bullshit artist who promises he can get you lots of gigs and make you a star.

I'll call this person R.G.

I met him at a pool party in Baltimore County thrown by a high school friend. R.G. was introduced to me as a comedian who also did magic. He was in his late 20's or early 30's. My friends had seen him perform at a club, loved him and invited him to the party.

R.G. and I hit it off from the beginning. We spent the evening making each other laugh. It was like great jazz – we were both riffing effortlessly and setting each other up, making everyone else laugh, too.

At the end of the night, he looked at me and said: "I'm not just saying this, but you're one of the funniest people I've ever met. And I want to help you. 'Cause you got it."

OK, maybe tiny alarm bells would be going off in your head at this point.

Maybe you'd be thinking: Hmmm, is this guy blowing smoke here or what?

But I guess I'm not that bright. Because I didn't hear any alarm bells at all.

A couple of weeks later, many of the same people at the pool party met at a bar in Timonium for a karaoke night. Again, R.G. was in attendance.

This time he took me aside and said: "I've got a big surprise for you. I have a friend who's a producer at FOX television. They're doing a special on young comedians in America. They're going to film some of it at the Lyric" – the venerable Baltimore mid-town theater – "and I got you a spot. It pays $500! And you're going to be on FOX!"

OK, maybe the alarm bells would be clanging even louder now for you.

Maybe they'd be accompanied by warning lights that flashed: RUN AWAY! RUN AWAY! WORLD-CLASS BULLSHIT!

But again, I saw nothing amiss.

In fact, if there was any kind of internal monologue going on in my head, it went like this:

Well, of course, this is how it's supposed to happen! My whole life will be like this! Of course, on a karaoke night in Timonium, some fucking magician I met at a pool party is going to give me the break of a lifetime and put me on national television!

Because I'm the funniest person in the world!

This is my destiny!

Anyway, upon hearing this blessed news from R.G., I went crazy.

I called my parents with the news. I called my friends. I called everyone I've ever known in my entire life. "I'M GOING TO BE ON FOX. WOO-HOO! "

It got even better. At a subsequent meeting with R.G., he told me the FOX people would be filming on such and such a date. He told me I needed to have a certain amount of material ready. I wrote all this down. I asked sensible questions. God, this was going to be great!

Now the big day is looming. I'm pumped and ready for my close up.

Except . . . the day before, I get a phone call. It's R.G.

"The gig has been postponed," he says. "But don't worry. It's definitely gonna happen."

A short while later, he gives me a new date for the filming. But at the last minute, he calls with more bad news: that gig's been cancelled, too.

OK, now the alarm bells are clanging like it's a 50-story building on fire. The man is definitely playing some kind of head-game here.

But to what end?

He's not getting any money from me. So why's he doing this? To impress me because he wants to be my manager? Why would I be impressed when the gigs keep falling through?

This goes on for weeks. Finally, of course, it's clear that no FOX comedy special will be forthcoming – at least none with Larry Noto in it.

Yet the whole time, R. G. keeps insisting that only bad luck has prevented me from dazzling the nation with my enormous comedic talent.

"I swear to you," he says over and over, "it just fell apart."

OK, at this point, I am through once and for all with R. G. Mercifully, I don't hear from him again.

Until . . . the phone rings a few weeks later.

It's R.G. again.

"I know that FOX thing fell apart," he says. "But you gotta believe me that it was legit. Anyway, I'm producing a comedy night at the Carney Crab House in Parkville. You can do 20 minutes. It pays 50 bucks."

OK, in my head, I know there's no reason to believe this guy. Except . . . the Carney Crab House is a legitimate place. This is probably more his speed than a network comedy special, I think. And sure enough, I find out it's a real show.

So I do the gig. I have friends from John Carroll show up to support me. Some of my former teachers are in the audience, too.

And I kill.

I play to a packed house downstairs. In fact, it goes so well that I do a half-hour instead of the 15 minutes I was supposed to do. Two other comedians go on after me, then R.G. goes on.

Except he bombs. He's rude to people. I don't like him. And I can see why the audience doesn't, either.

Now here comes another illuminating moment in my intro to the under-belly of comedy.

I'm standing in the back of the restaurant after my set, talking to the manager.

"You were really great," she says, and goes on to gush about my act.

Thanks, I say. Um, by the way, do I get paid by you? Or does R.G. pay me?

She gives me this funny look.

"What are you talking about?" she says. "The comedians aren't getting paid tonight. They're working for drinks."

My jaw drops.

Drinks?! I'm 18 years old! So what am I working for here, ginger ale?!

Luckily, before I go into a full-blown freak-out, I run into one of my old teachers. She's with her husband, a big guy who's a lawyer. When I relayed what the bar manager had just told me, the lawyer says: "Get R.G. to put it in writing that he owes you the money. And tell him you're taking him to small-claims court if he doesn't pay."

So I confront R.G. I tell him what the lawyer said. And R.G., he bullshits me to the very end.

"No, no," he says, "the manager said that because her father's handling the money. And he doesn't want her to know how much he's paying the comedians. I'll get you the money. I'll pay you later in the week."

Right. I'm going to fall for that?

What am I, a fucking idiot?

"Write what you just said on a piece of paper and sign it," I say. And he does.

Yet within minutes, he calls me over and hands me the cash that's owed me.

"Now give me that piece of paper," he says, and rips it up.

And that was the end of my dealings with R.G., a guy sleazy enough to try and take advantage of a kid just getting his feet wet in the business.

Unfortunately, he wouldn't be the last shark to circle around me in this business. But that's a story for a later chapter.

LARRY LIVE

The Airport

I was flying the other day . . . the boarding process was the most ridiculous thing I'd ever seen.

They have all these different groups now that dictate the order of who boards the plane first. Basically it's to hammer home just how important – or not important – you are to them.

"Now boarding . . . our elite members."

"Now boarding . . . our premium select members."

"Now boarding . . . our Willy Wonka Golden Ticket members."

For the elite members, they literally had a red carpet rolled out for them to board the plane. And as soon as they were boarded, they rolled up the red carpet, because God forbid us peasants walk on it, too!

I was in coach. By the time they got to us, they had actually smashed bottles on the ground so we had to walk over broken shards of glass to get on the plane.

I like flying Southwest because I like to see people get that confused over combining letters and numbers. It's a simple process, yet it baffles most people. The sign says A1-30, your pre-boarding slip says C42 – you don't belong here right now!

I like the fun nature of the Southwest flight attendants, too. They sing. They dance. They do magic tricks. It's all in good fun. I just hope they also know how to save us in an emergency. I'm just saying, when the plane is going down . . . I want more than a funny song about flight safety.

I like the sign at the security checkpoint that tells you not to make jokes about bombs, too. Was this a big problem? Were people really going up to the agents saying: "Knock, knock." "Who's there?" "I'm wearing underwear made of explosives?"

The new underwear screeners are a lot of fun. You know, the ones where you raise your hands, they scan you and you know everyone is judging you . . . I don't like to brag, but I went through once and the female agent slow-clapped and asked for my number.

CHAPTER 3

"THE LARRY NOTO SHOW"

In the fall of 1994, I went off to Loyola College. The small Jesuit school in north Baltimore was still a humble "college" back then, not a big-shot "university" like today.

Choosing Loyola would prove to be one of the best decisions I ever made in my life. I was a commuter. If my parents could have afforded to build a private monorail for me between Bel Air and the campus, believe me, they would have. But the love and support I got from the Loyola faculty and students over four years would set the foundation for much of what I would go on to accomplish in comedy – and also in life.

At Summer Orientation in August, an upper classman helping with the program – they were called Evergreens – noticed me making my fellow freshman laugh. And somehow word got around that I'd done stand-up comedy. As if my two modest gigs at Winchester's and an open-mic night in New York had suddenly turned me into Jerry Seinfeld.

Nevertheless, the Evergreens persuaded me to do some comedy at a mixer for freshman at a little campus coffee house called the Garden Garage. The place was packed that night. They introduced me and I took the stage.

And I was . . . *atrocious.*

I was extremely nervous – so nervous that I completely messed up a joke by saying the punch line when I hadn't finished the set-up.

The result was total silence. Crickets chirping. I was on for 10 minutes. It felt like an eternity.

I remember getting off the stage and thinking: Oh, my God, I have to go to Towson University! I have to transfer. This is the end of my Loyola career. I'm an incoming freshman and I've alienated myself before the goddamn school year has even started!

A guy named Chris Webb, a sophomore, came up to me afterward and said: "I know you probably think that didn't go well. But they're freshmen. They're too nervous to laugh, they don't know each other, etc. But I thought you were very funny."

Chris said my act had resonated with the upper-classmen in the room. He asked if I'd appear in an on-campus program called Iggies – a play on St. Ignatius of Loyola – that brought in entertainers to perform for the students.

I told him I didn't have enough material to do that kind of show. Then I mentioned how much I adored David Letterman and Johnny Carson. What if we did something patterned after a late-night TV talk show? I asked.

Chris was immediately intrigued.

"I've got contacts," he said. "I can help you get guests."

He said we'd put a program together, and we decided to call it "The Larry Noto Show." He got his roommate, who played guitar, and a couple of other buddies to be the house band. The format would be this: I'd come out and do a monologue, we'd have three guests and show a funny video.

My friend Tim Lavery, from Poughkeepsie, N.Y. – I would be the best man at his wedding in 2002 – would help me write and produce the shows. For the first video, which we shot in mid-December, we went to Towson Town Centre and I interviewed people and riffed off their responses.

Imagine a nervy college kid in a turtleneck, with sideburns thicker than shag carpeting, waving a microphone in the startled faces of holiday shoppers, and you have some sense of what went on.

The only advertising we did for the show was through word of mouth and flyers posted in each dorm. Nevertheless, on a cold December night, right before exams, "The Larry Noto Show" made its debut.

And damned if it wasn't an immediate hit.

In a tiny coffee house that normally attracted 15 or 20 students to the Iggies, we drew well over 150 people.

My monologue was OK, a few hits, a few misses. Our first guests were the faculty member in charge of student affairs, who was funny and terrific, as well as the president of the Student Government Association and the captain of the soccer team.

I did well with the interviews, was quick enough with the ad-libs and the video was a big hit. We got a lot of laughs – which was a relief because we thought it was so bad before the show we almost pulled it.

Overall, the show went great. I remember Chris, Tim and I sitting there in the empty coffeehouse when it was all over, practically in shock. We were like: *What just happened?* Chris was ecstatic.

"Well," he said, "we're obviously going to do this again."

And we did. We decided to do one show per month. They began after winter break. And now the guest format was this: one faculty guest, one student guest and one outside guest.

For our second show, we landed Darius Johnson, a star basketball player for Loyola. Johnson had hit the game-winning three-pointer against Manhattan a year earlier to lift the Greyhounds to their very first NCAA Tournament berth in Division I.

Yet the following season, after a conflict with a new coach, Johnson was off the team. No one knew exactly why. The player said he was forced off. The coach said the parting was by "mutual agreement."

Whatever the reason, it was a big story. The whole campus was talking about it. The Baltimore *Sun* newspaper was writing about it.

Snaring Johnson was a great coup for the show. I felt more like Mike Wallace of "60 Minutes" than David Letterman. And the feedback I got from faculty members was that I'd done an excellent job with the interview.

On that second show, we also did a take-off of "The Newlywed Game" called "The Professor Dating Game," where we peppered three sets of married professors about their dating habits before they were married.

The shows kept getting better and better. Student interest in them soared, too. And I was becoming something of a celebrity on campus. Faculty members were joking with me in class ("Are you *the* Larry Noto?") The president of Loyola, Father Harold "Hap" Ridley, was mentioning me in his speeches. He was also telling people that the school should change the sign on the Loyola bridge over Charles Street bridge to read: "Home of the Larry Noto Show."

We decided to move the final show of the year to McManus Theatre, the 300-seat venue where the college held its plays.

Chris Webb named it "The Larry Noto Show Year-End Spectacular." (Yes, we wanted to go subtle.) The show sold out. Musical entertainment was by the Smooths, a terrific ska band on campus. And the featured guest was the great Artie Donovan, the Hall of Fame defensive tackle for the old Baltimore Colts and all-around funnyman who had appeared on Letterman more than a dozen times.

I came on stage in a golf cart, doing my Letterman wave and gesturing to the band, and it brought down the house. Golf carts were the ubiquitous method of transportation for faculty members and staff on campus. In fact, my joke back then was: "I don't know whether I'm going to class or playing the back nine."

Artie was unbelievable. He was on autopilot the whole time, smiling and getting big laughs with his self-deprecating humor and wry observations. My friend Sergio Vitale's father, Aldo, brought cannolis. And – don't ask me why – we brought people on stage to fill the cannolis and throw them out to the audience.

Letterman gave out hams. We gave out cannolis.

The shows went on the following spring. Our guests ranged from the sublime to the downright quirky.

Bea Gaddy, the tireless advocate for the poor and homeless known as "the Mother Theresa of Baltimore," made an appearance. So did then-Baltimore councilman Martin O'Malley and Mike Aronin, a gifted comedian with cerebral palsy who played off his disorder to hysterical effect. (Mike would become a life-long friend and we'd work together as comics several times – including a corporate gig where we learned minutes before the show that the audience hardly spoke English.)

We brought in a Camden Yards vendor who had become a sensation with his loud, sing-song chants of "Ice cold icy Cokes! Ice cold icy-ice" during Orioles games. He showed up in full vendor regalia with a rack of soft drinks.

Also on that show was WMAR-TV sportscaster Keith Mills. This was right around the time that Orioles legend Cal Ripken Jr., had broken Lou Gehrig's record for consecutive games played.

It was our sixth show. We had a big number 5 hanging on the wall behind me. Midway through my monologue, our announcer Essam Shomali, pulled a string and number 6 took its place. It was a take-off of the iconic moment when the Orioles unveiled 2131 on the warehouse wall seconds after Cal's record-breaking feat.

When the show was over, Keith Mills gushed: "This is one of the best things I've ever seen – not just in college, but *anywhere!*"

It was high praise, and we were getting it from all over. The shows were that good, funny and fresh, with a vaguely anarchic feel to them. Tim Lavery would say later that they "didn't feel amateurish. It didn't feel like this (was) just a couple of kids horsing around."

The following year, for our one-year anniversary show, we moved to 600-seat McGuire Hall. Again, the show sold out. The headliner guest was Barry Williams, the former "Brady Bunch" star. He was in the midst of a "Growing Up Brady" national tour, supposedly spilling the secrets behind the making of the famous 1970s sitcom.

He was arrogant and condescending and gave me a hard time in the interview, trying to show he was the boss. But I handled him well. Tim Lavery recalled that after every smarmy comment from Williams, I'd look at the audience and make a face, which got a lot of laughs.

The only good memory I have of Barry Williams was that his manager watched the show from back-stage, pointed at me and remarked to someone nearby: "That kid's gonna be a star."

By the spring of my sophomore year at Loyola, the show was bigger than ever. We had souvenir T-shirts, cups and posters made up. We enlisted the help of Karen Strong to help pre-interview guests and Rich Sigler to work some video editing magic.

But the effort of putting together the show was beginning to wear on me – and wear on others, too.

It was hard to go from a big venue like McGuire Hall back to a small room like the Garden Garage and the attention the show was getting put a strain on the friendship I had with Tim, which was important to me.

Tim and I could always make each other laugh, usually before even getting the joke out. (Because the other guy always knew something was coming). We laugh to this day over the way one of us ordered Pico de Gallo at a Chili's. I can't even try to make it funny to you, but to Tim and I that phrase is a part of our friendship vernacular.

The success of the show also got me worrying that I wasn't getting enough respect as simply the show's funnyman anchor. Maybe, I thought, I should run for vice-president of student activities so I could have an impact on social affairs on campus. Maybe *then* people would take me more seriously.

The truth was, the show was going to my head. I actually began thinking: Oh, God, what if people beat me up? Maybe I even need a bodyguard!

I know it sounds crazy. But, again, this all seemed like part of some master plan for my destiny. After all, I was *supposed* to be famous, wasn't I? I was *supposed* to be a celebrity. Hadn't people been telling me that for years?

So here it was: I was on campus and before the end of my freshman year, we had a hit show! We're selling out the theater, and I'm interviewing people like Artie Donovan and Barry Williams and the school president is making a joke about me in every speech!

Looking back on it now, I definitely needed to take a break. So I ran for the social activities post in the Student Government Association and won. I began putting all my effort and energy into planning concerts, comedy shows and outdoor festivals for the school.

The last "Larry Noto Show" was held in McGuire Hall at the end of my sophomore year. David Wild, a contributing editor at Rolling Stone magazine, was the featured guest. I had a vague notion of doing one show per semester going forward, but even that seemed daunting.

The larger feeling was this: I had done everything I could with the show and there was only more of the same thing ahead, and that would be boring. It sounds funny to say, but at age 19, I was ready for a new challenge. I wanted to see what else I could achieve.

Over my final two years at Loyola, I never did another show. It remains one of the biggest regrets of my life. But as I discovered some 20 years later, the show had a legacy that endured.

In 2014, I was part of a group of prominent alumni invited back to school for a mixer put on by the Communications department.

Walking around the campus, past the bridge over Charles Street and the Garden Garage and places where we had shot our videos, memories of "The Larry Noto Show" came flooding back.

I toured the facilities with a guy named Alan Danzis. Alan had started his own campus TV show in the 90's, a few years after "The Larry Noto Show" had run its course. Danzis' show had been called "Fate Date." Somehow he would convince two students to go out on a date and allow him to film the whole thing. It was a daring show for its time and a precursor to the reality TV craze that would eventually sweep the country.

Both of us were amazed at the full-blown TV studio, professional cameras and editing bays that students had access to now. At one point, we came upon a sophomore who happened to be editing a show.

When I was introduced, his eyes lit up.

"Oh," he said, "you're *that* Larry Noto?!"

Wait a minute . . . this kid had heard of me?

It made me feel like I was Jack Paar.

Paar was one of the early pioneers of NBC's "The Tonight Show," the witty host specializing in observational humor and dissecting American culture.

Me, I had helped bring an updated version of that to Loyola. So feeling like a talk-show icon – that was definitely something I could live with.

And I do to this day.

P.S. I attribute most of it to the cannolis.

LARRY LIVE

Snow Globes

Speaking of flying, the liquid restrictions are one of the worst rules if you just want to bring carry-on. I guess they're afraid you're going to shampoo someone to death during the flight.

And you KNOW the bad guys are going to find a work-around. No liquids? No problem. No shoes? OK, we'll get around that, too. They'll come up with some James Bond device we haven't thought of. But us? We have to suffer. I don't get to bring MY conditioner on the plane, MY hair looks bad the whole trip . . . and the terrorists win.

Did you know the no-liquid rule applies to snow globes?

I didn't either. But goddammit, I found out.

Apparently, trying to bring a Mickey Mouse snow globe home from Walt Disney World is one of the Top 10 signs you're about to join Al-Qaeda!

First is if you show an affinity for training on monkey bars. Seconds is the Mickey Mouse snow globe. And third is if you shout "Death to America!" instead of "Bingo!" when you win on a straight line.

I'm NEVER searched before boarding a plane, by the way. And it's always a little disappointing. They're patting down wheel chair bound grandmas. A little girl with a lollipop is getting water-boarded with Kool-Aid.

But me?

"Come on through, sir. You're harmless. You wouldn't hurt a fly."

So before a recent flight from Orlando, I'm breezing through the checkpoint.

"Need to see my license?" "No, come on through."

"I forgot my boarding pass." "We trust you. Pick any flight."

"I killed a man in Korea." "I'm sure he had it coming. Keep moving, please."

But this time, something different happened. I put my items on the belt. Shoes. iPad. Carry-on case. A Disney shopping bag with mementos from the trip.

Everything was going smoothly. I think the agent even sped the belt up at one point. My ability to be a threatening male in society was being dismissed one item at a time.

Then something happened . . .

The belt stopped. Not slowed – STOPPED. It even backed up a bit. And stopped again. And people huddled! Agents! Certified security authorities! They gathered!

I was causing a conversation! A discussion! Analysis! Maybe even an international crisis! It was magical!

Until, of course, I found out what the problem was . . .

The agent approached me slowly. My Mickey Mouse snow globe was in one of her hands.

"Sir, is this snow globe yours?" she asked.

"Yes. Yes, it is," I said, more than a little disappointed.

THIS IS WHY I'M BEING STOPPED?! THIS is going to bring me down? THIS is what they'll be discussing tonight on CNN? What about that guy in Korea?

"You can't take this on the plane," the agent said. "Because of the water inside the globe."

I looked at her. "What am I supposed to do?"

"You're going to have to check it."

Check it?! CHECK THE SNOW GLOBE? How the hell am I supposed to check a snow globe?

Can you imagine me at the baggage carousel after the flight . . . and all the bags are going by . . . and here comes my fucking little snow globe on the belt?

And I better check the tag to make sure it's MY snow globe, since they all look alike.

No, forget that. I told the agent I wasn't going to check it, and that I guessed she could just keep it.

"Sir, are you surrendering the snow globe?" she asked.

"I surrender the snow globe!" I said as I slowly walked away with my hands in the air.

But . . . how on earth am I gonna hijack a plane with a snow globe?

What am I gonna do – mesmerize everyone with the little floating flakes?

Just hop up in the middle of the flight and yell: "Alright everybody!" and slowly walk up and down the aisle, methodically shaking my snow globe? Watching people freeze in terror at the sight of the little snowflakes falling over Mickey Mouse in a taunting manner? The flakes swirling more and more violently with each shake of my hand?

And with my deranged stare letting everyone know I'm in charge and conveying a threat too horrible to voice out loud, but that's clearly on everyone's mind:

"Don't make me turn the crank and play the music . . ."

CHAPTER 4

A SMALL TASTE OF THE BIG TIME

Near the end of my sophomore year at Loyola, I was walking in the quad when a professor named Toni Keane stopped me.

"Hey," she said, "you're that kid with that show."

Guilty as charged. Uh, unless you don't like the show. In which case, I'm not that kid.

But apparently she was a fan. Because in the next breath, she told me about a guy named Dan Rodricks, a Baltimore *Sun* columnist who had a live weekend talk/entertainment show on WMAR-TV, the local ABC affiliate. It was called "Rodricks for Breakfast."

"You're really funny and you guys have similar personalities," she said. "You should call him."

Call him?

Me?

Well, OK.

Actually, this would prove to be a recurring theme in my life: people randomly popping up to help me, either by offering advice or giving me a chance or doing something so kind to further my career that it truly touched me.

I was still doing "The Larry Noto Show" at the time. When I called WMAR, it was actually to see whether Dan would be a guest on my show, or whether I could be a guest on his show.

That went nowhere.

Then I asked about an internship.

Bingo!

"Come in one day and watch us edit," Will Schwarz, Dan's producer, said. "Then you can sit in and watch the show."

I did just that, and the hustle and bustle of the station's newsroom was intoxicating. Working all around me were Ch. 2 personalities like Stan Stovall, Mary Beth Marsden, Jamie Costello and Keith Mills, people I'd watched and admired for years.

Sitting with director Keith Nelson as "Rodricks for Breakfast" aired was amazing, too. Staring at a wall of TV screens, Keith calmly called for different camera shots while monitoring preparations for the next segment, bringing the show in and out of commercial breaks and listening to Dan in one ear.

The total effect was like watching a talented conductor lead a symphony orchestra.

I got the internship and immediately fell in love with the show, which was quirky and fun and celebrated all things Baltimore.

On one of my first assignments at a duckpin bowling alley, I watched our cameraman, Peter Kulsziski, take off his shoes, pick up his camera and run down the alley in his socks, holding the camera around his ankles before crashing wildly into the pins.

No, he hadn't flipped out – he was just shooting one of the "bumps" that took us in and out of commercial breaks.

But the show was also a great vehicle for spirited conversation, the topics running from the tragic school shootings at Columbine to the death of Frank Sinatra to how the Orioles and Ravens were doing.

It was show biz. It was energy. It was action.

I couldn't get enough of it!

In my three years doing the show, I rose from intern to field producer, then to associate producer, and finally to one of the producers.

That show kindled my love affair with Baltimore. I got to meet all these great characters – some higher than other on the weirdo quotient. And I got to visit all these off-the-beaten-path places I would have never discovered on my own.

On a single show, I could be in a garage in the working-class Hampden neighborhood, watching a guy make flowerpots out of old tires. Then a few minutes later, I'd be zooming to the Cross Street Market downtown to mic Mayor Kurt Schmoke so we could talk about the city's gun buy-back program. And in between, I'd be driving around in the WMAR van like a big shot with cameramen like Tommy "Ring-A-Ding-Ding" Wynkoop, talking about movies, Sinatra and girls.

Before long, in addition to my producing and writing roles, I was making regular on-air appearances.

I was a movie fanatic, so Dan let me do movie reviews and bits where I'd try to guess the winners of the Oscars or talk about what films would be hot at the box office that summer.

When baking mogul and multi-millionaire developer John Paterakis proposed building a convention hotel a mile from the actual convention center in Baltimore, Dan found the idea to be ludicrous.

So on a broiling summer day, he had me impersonate a typical conventioneer and walk from the convention center to the proposed hotel site in a dark blue business suit while toting a briefcase.

Back in the studio, Dan would check in on me at regular intervals as I huffed and sweated my way along Pratt Street, trying to stave off heat stroke.

Then there was our spoof of the "Blair Witch Project," the horror movie about three film students who venture into a Maryland forest to shoot a documentary on a local witch legend, only to disappear, leaving just their footage to tell the tale.

Our version, which I wrote with Reagan Warfield (who would

go onto fame at Baltimore radio station MIX- 106.5), was called the "Blair Road Project." This was a send-up of the way Baltimoreans pronounced Bel Air Road, a major city thoroughfare, as "Blair" Road. So we did a faux-spooky bit – complete with jerky camera shots and breathless narration – about three young people heading off into the woods to find the missing "e" from "Blair."

That was the beauty of Dan's show. You could be creative and try things you couldn't dream of trying on other local TV programs.

Everything I did on the show wasn't light or funny, though. The very first package Dan gave me to produce was about Joshua's Lighthouse Angels, a tiny shop in Hampstead, Md., run by a woman named Mary Dansicker.

She had created a memory wall dedicated to her son Joshua Dansicker, a 21-year-old college senior killed in a car accident. Mary was encouraging people who had lost a child to come to the store to mourn and reflect. They could also post a message on angel-shaped paper – one read only "See you on the other side" – and tape it to the wall as a form of healing.

Here I was, only 21 years old, talking to this tearful woman about death and grieving and feeling in way over my head. But I put the piece together and it aired and Mary Dansicker loved it. She even sent a letter to the station' manager expressing how perfectly the piece had captured her story.

Eventually, it was even nominated for an Emmy by the National Academy of Television Arts and Sciences. It didn't win. But that was okay, because there was nothing like getting approval from Dan that signaled you'd done a great piece for the show.

I was still doing the Rodricks show on the weekends when I graduated from Loyola and got a job at Stanton Communications, a PR firm whose Baltimore office was headed by a genial man named Ray Weiss. But five months later, I was offered an entry-level job at HBO in New York, where I had interned two summers earlier.

What followed was the most agonizing decision of my young life.

All sorts of thoughts ran through my head. Taking the job would mean moving to the Big Apple, of course. Sure, there were exciting and glamorous aspects to that. But I wondered: how are you going to survive in New York making $30,000 a year?

I asked myself: is this how the journey of happiness begins? And what *is* happiness? Isn't it about quality of life?

Do I suffer in a shitty little Manhattan apartment and sell the beautiful new fire-engine-red Mustang I'd just bought? (Oh, did I love that car!) Do I want to ride the subway every day? Do I want to be away from my family and friends?

I even sat down with a career counselor at Loyola, Mary DeManns, who had me list the pros and cons of taking the job. "This is one of the toughest decisions I've ever seen anyone have to make," she said.

In the end, I didn't take the job. Maybe some of it was fear-based. Was I good enough and smart enough to work for HBO and move up the ranks? Was I up to the challenge of carving out a new life in New York? (Which might as well have been Vancouver for a guy who couldn't even drive to Baltimore.)

But most of it was me thinking: I'm gonna be a big fish in a small pond in Baltimore. And I'm OK with that. I'm working for a great guy, I'll still do the Rodricks show, it'll be a good life.

Except . . . "Rodricks for Breakfast" went off the air a year later.

Even though the ratings were good, management had decided it was getting too expensive to produce. When we went off the air, I had risen to co-producer, the position I'd held in such awe when I first started as an intern. We all cried when the show was over. What a loss it was to Baltimore and for me personally. My creative outlet was gone.

It was also my first sense that maybe this grand plan I'd envisioned for my career wasn't always going to go smoothly.

Yet in a way I was still optimistic, because the general manager of WMAR, Drew Barry, loved me. Even though the show was ending, there was talk of me assuming other roles at the station.

Producing an investigative show was mentioned. So was working on one of the specials Dan had purportedly agreed to host.

But nothing really materialized.

Finally, I was offered a job on the station's assignment desk. But I turned that down, too. And that decision was easy. I was way too young and ambitious to live my life listening to police and fire scanners.

The other thing that made the decision easy was my realization that local TV – and radio, for that matter – was a tough, crappy business.

Ken Phillips, the affable long-time meteorologist for WMAR, had just been abruptly fired after 17 years with the station. And Steve Rouse, for 17 years the popular host of the morning show "Rouse & Company" on radio station WQSR, had been fired so suddenly after a format change that he never even had a chance to say good-bye to his listeners.

I realized you didn't control your own destiny in those jobs. No, those were ruthless, bottom-line folks doing the hiring and firing there.

And I wasn't about to put my happiness – and my destiny – in the hands of those kinds of people.

LARRY LIVE

Passion of the Christ

My father watched "The Passion of the Christ" the other day.

Now I know the movie has been out for quite some time. But the man has only been in the country for 50 years, so he's just figured out how to work the "movie machine" as he calls it.

My dad is the kind of guy who finds fault in everything. There's always SOMETHING to complain about.

So you normally don't . . . talk to him.

But I made the mistake and asked him: "Dad, heard you watched 'Passion of the Christ.' What'd you think?"

"Good movie," he replied. "Good movie . . ."

And in my head, I'm thinking: "Wait for it . . . wait for it . . ."

And sure enough, he says: "Except . . . yeah . . . I didn't really care for that lead guy . . ."

WHO??? JESUS?!?!

Who watched "The Passion of the Christ" and didn't have passion for Christ?!

Who DID you like in this film?

Not only that, but my dad was watching the "Director's Cut." Like he thought it was going to be different than the original version.

I don't know . . . how do you change this film? Maybe Jesus makes it this time?

Maybe He hops off the cross and beats the shit out of everyone . . . running in slow motion as the cross bursts into flames behind him . . .

"I don't remember that from the book . . ."

Any time I talk about that film, I'm reminded of where I saw it.

Which was in the theater.

On a date.

It could explain why I don't get lucky on a regular basis. I'm not planning the dates too well . . .

I don't care how good your game is – there is no move you make after watching "The Passion of the Christ" that's gonna work.

We just sat in the car and confessed our sins to each other when it was over.

You're basically prayer buddies at that point.

You're not going to visit any bases with that girl – just Stations of the Cross.

CHAPTER 5

CHARMING 'EM IN CHARM CITY

At Stanton Communications, I was doing PR for a number of different clients, including the Baltimore Association for Retarded Citizens, the Arthritis Foundation, and the National Federation for the Blind.

The work was hard. But the truth was, it was a great job. And Ray Weiss was a great boss. He gave me wonderful advice. As a PR person, he said, you have two clients: the clients who are paying us and the media. And you need to treat the media as a client as well. Because if you treat them well and deliver for them, you'll be very successful in this business.

I never forgot that.

When the National Federation for the Blind sued America On Line – now AOL, the multinational mass media corporation – claiming the Americans with Disabilities Act (ADA) should apply to the blind who wanted access to the service's email and other options without needing the help of a sighted person, I flew to Boston with the team and did all the press releases and helped with the news conference announcing the lawsuit.

I was all of 23 years old, and this was heady stuff. I learned the craft of PR quickly. And I became pretty good at it.

When my friend Sergio Vitale and his family opened a new groundbreaking restaurant in Baltimore's Little Italy called Aldo's Ristorante Italiano, I did the publicity. I found out "The Best Of" show hosted by Marc Silverstein on The Food Network was doing a holiday special. I pitched Aldo's to be featured on the show and they accepted.

Problem was: it wasn't anywhere near the holidays. It was early September.

But we decorated Aldo's as if it were Christmas, even putting wreaths and candles in the windows. Invited guests, mainly family and friends, showed up in red sweaters. The segment featured the traditional Italian Christmas Eve Feast of the Seven Fishes. Everyone dined, laughed, Sergio sang opera. And at the end of the night, the staff and the production crew all sat around telling stories and drinking wine.

It may have been late summer outside, but it truly did feel like a family celebration of Christmas Eve inside.

Aldo's would go on to be featured by *Southern Living* magazine and *The New York Times* and become one of the most acclaimed restaurants in the city.

Soon after, an epic drought hit Baltimore. The drought was all over the news. It was all anyone was talking about.

One day, Sergio attended a restaurant association meeting and called me afterward.

"I don't know if this is anything or not," he began. "But we decided to stop serving tap water during the drought. We're going to give customers a complimentary bottle of water instead."

We immediately started brainstorming. Sergio and I had worked together in student government at Loyola and were close friends. I was always in awe of his natural business sense and his knowledge of the restaurant industry. And we had one other big thing in common

– we were both fascinated with how the media worked.

"That's a story!" I practically shouted about the water bottle give-away.

I contacted every media outlet in town. When I was done, the story made the *Sun.* It was also on every radio station in town.

 Best of all, WBAL-TV, the local NBC affiliate, went live from Aldo's with their lead story that night: "What restaurateurs are doing to help battle the drought!"

This included footage of the friendly wait-staff telling diners how much Aldo's valued its relationship with area farmers – so much so that it would serve complimentary bottles of water rather than use precious tap water that would further endanger the drought-stricken area and hurt the farmers even more.

Pure genius, baby! You couldn't buy that kind of publicity no matter how much you spent. To me, it's still one of my greatest PR coups.

In 1999, I left Stanton to take a job with Visit Baltimore, the official marketing organization whose mission was to attract convention, group, and leisure visitors to the city. (It was called B.A.C.V.A. – Baltimore Area Convention and Visitors Association – back then, but changed later on because they were getting too many calls from people looking to order Greek desserts!)

I was charged with getting positive press for Baltimore as a travel destination. So I attended travel shows, worked with publications such as *Southern Living* and *The New York Times* and schmoozed travel writers on a daily basis in an effort to portray the city in the best possible light.

After working on a weeklong shoot with the Aer Lingus in-flight film crew, the producer wrote a letter to Mayor Martin O'Malley stating, "I have never met a person so committed to his job and his city. Baltimore needs people like Larry. I can say with absolute certainty that we have never experienced the level of quality and support and service that we received. Baltimore cared . . . and Larry Noto cares about Baltimore."

The mayor sent me a letter thanking me for my service to the city and when I ran into him on the sidelines of the Army-Navy game at M&T Bank Stadium, Mayor O'Malley smiled and said: "The Larry Noto Show . . . I still have my T-shirt!"

I went to Germany in conjunction with a trip by the Pride of Baltimore, the 19th-century reproduction of a clipper ship that served as a traveling good-will ambassador for the city. The ship was stopping in Hamburg, so we were doing a reception on the ship to talk up Baltimore to tour operators and the media.

It was my first trip to Europe. To say it didn't begin well is an understatement.

My boss, Dan Lincoln, the VP of marketing, was supposed to go with me and show me the ropes. Except he never showed up the airport. He was still not there as the flight began boarding.

I didn't know what to do.

Do I get on the plane? Do I not get on the plane? Dan was Mr. World Traveler, the guy who was supposed to show me what to do. Eventually I got on the plane. But I was a nervous wreck.

As I settled into my seat, an announcement came over the PA system: "Is there a Mr. Larry Noto on board?"

For an instant, I wanted to play the big shot. *Jesus Christ, I can't even get away for one minute without someone bothering me . . . !*

But I was too rattled for jokes.

A flight attendant handed me a piece of paper. It was a message from Dan. He was stuck in traffic. He would try to get on the next flight and meet me in Germany.

WHAT?!

Me in Germany . . . alone?!

Now I felt like Macaulay Culkin – only in reverse!

When we landed, I exchanged some money at the airport and took a cab to the hotel. But I had no idea what I was doing. I probably tipped the cab driver a thousand dollars. Thank God Dan landed five hours later.

That night at the reception, I was mingling with reporters when one asked: "How was your trip over?'

"It was a little bumpy," I replied.

"Yes," he said, "the waters can be a little choppy this time of year."

Which was when it occurred to me: he thought I had sailed over on the Pride!

I wanted to go off on him and say: "I flew over here, you moron! I wasn't sailing on the boat, heave-ho-ing like I'm a fucking pirate or something!"

But that probably wouldn't have been great for international relations. Not to mention it would have perpetually branded me in travel circles as the mouthy psycho from Visit Baltimore.

Still, all in all, this was a wonderful adventure for me. We spent one particularly memorable night drinking in the hotel bar with a huge, gregarious German and later the party moved to an Irish pub down the street.

At one point, Dan took me aside and said: "I want you to do me a favor. I want you to soak in this moment. I've been doing this for a while, and this is your first trip. When you're back in your office and it gets shitty and you're stressed, just close your eyes and come back to this place."

It was more terrific advice. I totally took it to heart.

I worked for Visit Baltimore for four years and had a ball. I traveled to London, Germany and Paris for the job, hosted dinners for the media back in Baltimore, arranged press tours. I became known as Mr. Baltimore for my enthusiastic promotion of the town. I got to watch reporters from all the country and the world experience the best the city had to offer and truly fall in love with Baltimore.

And even though I was doing public relations, I was using my comedic skills. Dinners. Networking events. Press tours. I treated them all like mini shows. I could answer questions, wine and dine, get laughs and hit my talking points all at the same time.

Eventually, things began to sour at work.

Visit Baltimore was going through a rough spell. Things got messy between the board and the mayor and the CEO, whom they eventually let go. Morale was horrible. My colleagues were whispering in the hallways about their jobs.

It was a tough year, like watching your best friend die.

But you know what they say: when the going gets tough, the tough . . . start looking for another job.

I didn't have to look too far. Ken Conklin was the general manager for Harbor Magic, a consortium of boutique hotels in Baltimore. Ken had a great creative, marketing mind and was focusing on the hotel group's destination experience.

Ken and I would have great dinner conversation about Disney and how the best marketing was a great experience. When the timing was right, we had lunch, wrote some details on a napkin and I became the director of marketing.

In the meantime, though, something else wonderful happened.

In 2002, the Baltimore Improv opened.

And I started to hope again.

LARRY LIVE

Italian Nicknames

When people find out my father was born in Sicily, they automatically assume we're part of the Mob.

"You're from Italy? So, you're like the Sopranos, huh?"

No, we're not part of the Mob, people! I hate that stereotype. And I swear, the next person who says that to me, I'm gonna have them whacked.

There ARE some similarities between my family and Mafia, though.

You know how the Mob has nicknames for everyone?

"Lemme introduce you to the crew here . . . this is Tony the Chin . . . Vinnie the Killer . . . Tommy the Greek . . ."

Well, my family does the same thing.

The other night, my mother says:

"Yeah, we had dinner at your Uncle Charlie's . . . you know, Uncle Charlie, the cheap bastard . . . He's married to your Aunt Marie, the drunk . . . they got that daughter Laura, the whore . . ."

And the older they get, they don't even remember the nicknames anymore.

If you're having a conversation with my grandmother about one of our relatives, you're like a contestant on the "$25,000 Pyramid." The woman is just throwing out clues.

"The one who walks with a limp . . . the one who spits when he talks . . ."

I'm yelling: "I don't know . . . people who were at Thanksgiving? People named Uncle Vinnie?"

BING!

CHAPTER 6

THE OPPORTUNITY OF A LIFETIME

I was in a meeting at Visit Baltimore when I heard the Improv was coming to Power Plant Live!, the collection of bars and clubs nestled directly across from the Inner Harbor.

"This is it!" I said to myself.

Doing standup had always been in the back of my mind, dating back to my first halting gigs at Winchester's and the New York Comedy Club. I just hadn't had an outlet.

But this . . . *this* was finally my big chance

The Improv was the Rolls Royce of comedy clubs, too. It attracted A-list comics. Now it had actually come to my backyard!

I laughed. I cried. It was better than "Cats."

Not long after opening, the Improv held a contest to find "The Funniest Person in Baltimore."

It was all bullshit: the initial rounds of the contest hinged on audience votes, rather than any impartial judging by anyone who knew comedy. Which meant it could be rigged if you got enough audience members to vote for you.

Hell, I thought, *I'm* funny. And since I knew everyone in town, I could rig the crowd with the best of them. You want to see *rigged*?! I'll show you rigged!

So I promoted my appearance to everyone I knew and was beyond touched when something like a 100 people showed up. These were all tourism industry professionals I knew from the National Aquarium, the Science Center and Harborplace, as well as colleagues from Visit Baltimore.

Even though I wasn't really super-nervous for my very first gig at a legendary Improv, I affected a neurotic delivery in the spirit of Woody Allen and Richard Lewis, two of my comedy heroes. But don't get me wrong: I was up in front of a big crowd and my adrenaline was definitely pumping.

I did seven minutes, including a bit about how Italians say the same thing at weddings and funerals – only the tone is different. ("Hey, she looks good, doesn't she?").

I got some big laughs and continued to survive the elimination rounds, thanks in no small part to my legion of, ahem, unbiased supporters.

In the end, though, I failed to place in the top three. A lot of people thought I was robbed. But the manager of the Improv, Dan Tracy, told me I was funny and promised to book me soon, which he never did.

I started going to more and more open mic nights to work on material and my delivery. Friends like Tracey Harrington McCoy and Alex Ball would come with me for support and even help me flesh out some of the jokes. I'm required by law to state here that Alex wrote the last line in my infamous "Law and Order" routine (which is presented in this book for your comedy pleasure.)

Undeterred, I entered the "Funniest Person in Baltimore" contest again the following year. (Hey, they weren't getting rid of me that easily.) This time I made it to the finals and *killed*. When I walked off the stage, I thought: *you may have just won this thing*.

But by the time I turned the corner, a young comic named Erik

Myers was lighting up the room. He was this real skinny kid with a shrill voice that sounded like Donald Duck being fed through a wood-chipper. And he did a lot of stoner-type jokes.

"The other day I fell asleep on the toilet," he said. "Only problem was, I was at the Outback Steak House."

It was totally different from any of the other acts – especially mine, which was now pretty clean. Erik was very funny, too. Within seconds, I thought: *He'll win for sure.*

And he did. I placed third. I thought to myself: Hmmm, two accidental deaths and that title is mine, baby.

When I walked off the stage after the voting totals were announced, the new manager of the Improv, Tara Lynn, came up to me.

"You're good," she said. "Why the fuck aren't you performing at this club?"

Go ask your buddy Dan Tracy, I said. He promised to book me for months.

But within days, Tara called me with great news.

"Brian Regan's coming to town," she said. "You're clean, and I need a clean comic to pair with him. I'd like to book you with him for eight shows over four nights."

I was ecstatic – this would be my first real paid gig as a comic! And I'd be opening for Brian Regan!

OK, the truth was, I didn't really know who Brian Regan was. But other comics knew him – and loved his act. Maybe he wasn't a household name, but he was definitely big-time. And his rep was growing every day.

Watching Brian Regan was like watching a master at work. Every show was sold out. We did one show Thursday night, three Friday night, three Saturday night, and one Sunday night. And he was still doing "A" material Sunday that he hadn't done any other night!

Like material you'd *kill* to have! And for him, it was probably his 700th bit of the weekend. Ho-hum.

I was so nervous the first night that I almost forgot his name when introducing him. Actually I *did* forget it at first.

"Ladies and gentlemen," I began, "are you ready for your head-liner?" Which is when it occurred to me: *I can't remember the guy's name!*

I ad-libbed with the crowd for a few seconds ("Are you excited?!"), frantically trying to summon the name. I was almost going to use that old show-biz announcer cliché and shout: "SO WHO ARE YOU HERE TO SEE?"

But finally his name popped into my head. Disaster narrowly averted. The intro went off fine.

Brian Regan was so clever and inventive that I sat there in awe when he took the stage. He did three or four hysterical minutes about trying to invent an ironing board that didn't make that squeaky *EEEEIII!* sound when you opened it.

I've ironed every day of my life. And I *never* would have thought of that bit.

Watching him, there was a part of me that said: there's no reason for me to do comedy. Because this guy is the master. This guy is great. I'm never gonna be this guy. What am I gonna say that he hasn't already heard?

But that was the wrong view to take at the time – I realize it now. Because when you're young and you're trying to find material, well, OK, what's been done? It's *all* been done! You have to come up with your own stuff, and put your own spin on it.

Brian Regan couldn't have been nicer in the green room between shows.

He gave me some good advice, mainly that I needed to slow down my delivery. One thing I learned over the years is that silence is a very scary moment for a comedian. But sometimes you need it – partic-ularly with a joke where you're asking the audience to think for a moment.

Brian also told me that you don't always need a transition between jokes. It's perfectly OK to tell a joke, pause, and go on to another joke.

Then he passed along a tip the great Rodney Dangerfield had given him: write the joke as if you're saying it, then black out whatever words aren't necessary for it to be funny.

Keep it lean and mean.

The weekend flew by – I felt like I was walking on air. But it also set the stage for me to become spoiled. Let's face it: by rights, a young comedian's first weekend gig should not be with the terrific Brian Regan at the Improv.

No, it usually works like this: you go out and you play these shit-shows at these open-mic nights and bars and fire halls and American Legion posts on a Tuesday night, and maybe you do this for years.

You don't get Brian Regan at a top-tier sold-out club with audiences that are smart and know comedy.

Maybe I didn't know how lucky I was at the time.

But I sure do know it now.

LARRY LIVE

The Bus Ad

I saw the most bizarre ad on the side of a bus the other day. You know how they have those big ads on buses?

This one said: SYPHILIS.

Right there. In giant letters. Cruising down a city street.

And underneath SYPHILIS it said:

IS 30 MINUTES OF FUN WORTH A LIFETIME OF PAIN?

Can you believe that? Is that bizarre or what?

I mean . . . 30 MINUTES!?

You know, if your fun is lasting 30 minutes, maybe it IS worth a lifetime of pain.

But I guess it shouldn't surprise anyone that we have advertisements for syphilis now, because we have commercials for everything in this country.

What I don't understand is when I see a commercial for a product that we've already accepted as part of our society.

Like plastic.

Yes, the plastic industry is spending millions of dollars on TV commercials trying to convince you and me that plastic is a good thing.

Helloooo?! It's PLASTIC! I'm pretty sure we're all on board.

It's not like plastic just showed up in this country. It's been around since, what, 1907?

Then we have commercials for food products that have been around for a million years.

"BEHOLD THE POWER OF CHEESE!" and "GOT MILK?"

Are there really people out there who haven't heard of these things yet?

Is there a guy at home watching TV with a dry bowl of Froot Loops going: "Huh? Milk?"

As he slowly puts each Froot Loop into his mouth by hand, amazed at this new "milk" thing he's hearing about?

CHAPTER 7

THE GREAT DOM IRRERA

The weekend with Brian Regan was both exhilarating and surreal. Sometimes I had to pause and ask myself: Did that really just happen?! Was that really you up there opening for a major comic in front of a packed house in your hometown?!

As I walked out of the Improv after our final gig together, I gazed at the big black-and-white photos in the lobby of the upcoming acts.

One was of Dom Irrera, a classic comedian I've loved and admired since I was a kid. He was playing the Improv in two weeks.

My God, I thought, could you imagine working with Dom Irrera? That would be amazing.

Two days later, my phone rang. It was Tara Lynn.

"Great job with Brian," she said. "Hey, I'd like you to open for Dom Irrera."

WHAT?!

Doo-doo, doo-doo, doo-doo, doo-doo . . . OK, now this was getting spooky.

At the very least, it was starting to feel like something out of a corny Hollywood movie. You know the one: kid has a life-long dream and all of a sudden someone – a genie, a wizard, Santa, Donald Trump – pops into his life to make his dream come true.

Did Tara Lynn have that kind of juice?

That kind of mystical power?

Here I thought it would be six or eight months before I'd ever get another gig at the Improv.

And now they were letting me open for a comedy legend?

One of my childhood idols?

Was I being punked here?

Would I show up at the Improv on the big night, only to have a camera crew descend on me and an announcer with a big Chiclets smile thrust a microphone in my face and say: "C'mon, Dom Irrera? You didn't really think that was gonna happen, right?"

But, no, this was really happening.

Of course, about five minutes after Tara called, I started worrying about something else. (Worry, you may have guessed, is sort of my default mode.)

Now what I worried about was this: Dom Irrera did a lot of Italian jokes. A lot of observations about growing up in an Italian-American family in Philadelphia. Me, I did a lot of stuff about growing up Italian-American in Maryland.

Would he be upset if we were on the same bill and I opened with Italian jokes, too?

After agonizing about this for a few days, I asked the Improv managers to get in touch with one of his representatives.

"No, you're fine," the rep said. "As long as you're not doing his bits . . ."

Who, me?

Do Dom's bits?

I wasn't even sure I could do *my* bits, never mind someone else's.

So two weeks after opening for Brian Regan, here I am, back on stage at the Improv. I'm warming up the crowd for Dom, doing my eight or 10 minutes and wondering what he's going to be like when I finally meet him.

A few minutes into my act, I see him walk across the back of the room. Now I'm even more nervous than I was before.

I finally get off the stage, the second comedian goes on and Dom comes up to me.

This is it! I think. This is the big moment! I'm about to meet the great Dom Irrera!

Which is when he scowls at me and says: "What, are you doing my fucking act?"

OK, I'm mortified.

No, I'm *beyond* mortified. What's beyond mortified? So stunned and embarrassed you want to die? Or shoot yourself?

Yes, that's what I was at that moment.

Holy shit! Does Dom really think I stole his stuff?

I try to croak out a response.

But suddenly Dom smiles and says "Come here, you!" and grabs my cheeks. Then he hugs me.

My knees almost buckled.

Oh, my God, Dom was playing with me! He was breaking my balls!

In that instant, I went from scared comic to hugely relieved fellow comic. But as I was to learn the more I was around him, no one could keep a straight face and say things to throw you like Dom could.

In fact, he got me again the very next night.

We were hanging out in the green room before he went on. By this time, I was growing a little more comfortable with him. I think he was feeling the same way about me.

So I decided to go for broke.

I asked him for advice on how I could improve my act.

"You know," he said, appearing to give it some thought, "you're doing a great job. But you might want to add a few, you know, *jokes*."

Again, I didn't know what to think at first.

Was he being serious? Did he think my act sucked?

That I wasn't funny enough?

Was he one of these veteran comedians who believed in being brutally honest – no matter how much it hurts – when a young comic asks for tips?

But seconds later, he smiled, letting me know he was busting my chops again.

I saw him do that to other people new to the business, too — another reason why I never took it personally.

"You know what I like about you?" he'd say to a rookie comic, totally deadpan. "A lot of the comedians, they go for the humor. But you don't. You're above that."

It was always Dom being Dom.

Dom playing with your head, gently teasing you, doing that "we kid because we love" shtick. And once you knew where he was coming from, it made you feel great. Like you were a fraternity brother or something.

At one point during the weekend, Dom said: "Hey, my agent wants me to audition for 'The Sopranos.' I'm supposed to practice this script. Would you help me read the lines?"

This, of course, was a great chance for me to give him a taste of his own medicine.

I should have said: "Listen, Dom, I'm a little busy, OK? I gotta do eight minutes on stage tonight, my friend. While you sit back here and coast."

But I wasn't gutsy enough to try that yet.

Instead, he made me a copy of the script and I sat there reading the other characters' lines while he rehearsed his own. And the whole time I'm thinking: "How cool is this? Running 'Sopranos' lines for Dom Irrera in the green room!?"

Those back-to-back gigs with Brian Regan and Dom Irrera would be the beginning of a spectacular two-year run at the Improv for me, the two greatest years of my life.

A few weeks later, I'd get to open for yet another of the icons on my personal comedy Mount Rushmore.

And what I did to hang out with him became its own Improv legend.

LARRY LIVE

The Wedding Shower

I'm at that age when all my friends are getting married. Some of my friends are getting married for the SECOND time!

They're lapping me in marriage! They're getting second families faster than I can get second dates.

My one friend had what's called a Jack and Jill wedding shower. Which is the wedding shower for the women, but the men are allowed to come, too.

Like we've been begging to come to this? WHY? WHO INVENTED THIS?!

So you have to buy some fancy knife or pot that they've told you to buy for them and "surprise" them with it. And you have to go to the shower and pretend you're happy for them.

So I went.

The women had all these strange superstitions when they were opening the presents.

Like they said the number of ribbons you break when opening the presents equals the number of kids you'll have in the marriage.

Or if you open the present before reading the card, your second-born child will be cross-eyed and speak with a lisp.

Men don't have this – thank God.

It's not like we're at the bachelor party going: "Bob, Bob . . . if you don't stick your head between that stripper's breasts, your son won't be able to play baseball."

CHAPTER 8

DRIVING RICHARD LEWIS

I first saw Richard Lewis live on stage when the Baltimore Improv opened in 2001 – long before I ever performed there.

The place was sold-out that night. I went with my mother and our table was dead center, not far from the stage. I remember being so amped it was ridiculous.

See, Lewis was one of my comedy idols when I was growing up. He was great in "Robin Hood: Men in Tights" as the anxiety-ridden prince with the traveling cheek mole. I sat transfixed watching his HBO specials and his work on "Curb Your Enthusiasm."

I even read his book, "The Other Great Depression" about his countless addictions and dysfunctions and rocky quest for a spiritual life.

"I come from a long line of neurotics," went one of my favorite Lewis riffs. "My great-great-great-grandmother used to say to my great-great-great-grandfather: 'That's not how you load a cannon, you fucking idiot!'"

Or he'd talk about his parents worrying about him when he went on trips. Except they were so cheap that when he'd call collect to reassure them, he had to blurt, "The eagle has landed!" and hang up to avoid a charge.

How could you not love a guy who seemed to almost *vibrate* with that kind of sheer, existential angst?

OK, he's Jewish and I'm Italian. But it was like seeing my soul brother up-close and personal. And as Tony Soprano said, Italians are just Jews with better food. (That's right, I quote Tony Soprano the way some others quote Shakespeare.)

A young comic named Dave Siegel opened for Lewis that night at the Improv. When Siegel was finished, Lewis took the stage, shook the kid's hand and gushed: "How about that guy? Give it up for him! He's gonna be a big star!"

Taking in this scene in the noisy, darkened room, I was suddenly miserable. In fact, it almost killed me.

I thought: I've *got* to get on that stage.

See, I needed Richard Lewis to say I'm going to be a big star, too. I needed that kind of validation from someone with his stature in the business. Needed it like I need oxygen, if you want the truth.

OK, now fast forward a couple years. I'm 30 years old and a real, live working comedian myself. Hell, I've opened for Brian Regan and Dom Irrera! Still have my day job, but the Improv is booking me regularly, probably once a month at this point.

I'm loving life!

One day, apropos to nothing, I say to the Improv managers: "Look, if Richard Lewis ever returns, you've got to book me, too. That would be another dream gig."

The managers promise they'll keep that in mind.

And one day it actually happens. The managers call me in and say "Richard's coming. And we're giving you that weekend also."

Now I'm beside myself. This is going to be the greatest thing ever! Better than the Brian Regan weekend! Better than the Dom gigs!

I'm going to meet Richard Lewis!

I'm going to hang with him between shows, make him see how brilliant I am! Make him realize that I'm part of the next wave of dazzling young comics and maybe he'll, like, be my champion! Talk me up to some of the big shots in the biz! Get me some big-time gigs!

Hell, he might even tell me to come out to California and chill on the "Curb" set with him and Larry David!

Except . . . a week before the scheduled gig with Lewis, I get called by the Improv to emcee when the headliner cancels at the last minute and they shuffle the acts.

Right before the show, I'm in the green room with another young comic. The guy is tall, with dark hair. He looks eerily familiar.

Hey, I say, you're Dave Siegel! You opened for Richard Lewis here a couple years ago, right?

"Yep," he says. "Can you believe I didn't talk to him the whole weekend?"

What?! What does he mean? That he opened for him and didn't get to meet him??"

"But what about all the nice things he said about you?" I asked. "How you're gonna be a big star and all that?"

Siegel shakes his head.

"He never even saw my act," he says sadly. "Only interaction I had with him was a few seconds on-stage. He goes back to the hotel between shows."

Now I'm seriously bummed.

I'm going to get that close to Richard Lewis next week and not even *meet* him? He's going to spend time between sets scarfing down the chocolate mints on his hotel pillow instead of yukking it up with me?

We're not going to become BNFFs? (Best Neurotic Friends Forever.)

You gotta be kidding me!

Luckily, my bosses at the Improv are sympathetic to my plight. Not only that, but their collective brains start working overtime to solve the problem.

Finally one of them says: "Hey, what if you *drove* Richard Lewis?"

I look at him as if his head had just exploded.

"Yeah, that's it!" he continues. "We won't hire a car service for him, OK? You'll start the show, do your eight minutes, introduce the next act. Then you'll go pick him up at his hotel. Heck, you'll have plenty of time to get back and forth!"

Well.

This is the greatest idea I've ever heard in my life.

It's fucking *brilliant*!

And that's exactly the way it goes down.

The big weekend finally arrives and the plan goes into place. I do my act that first night, introduce the feature and hustle over to the Hyatt where Richard is staying.

I call him on the house phone.

"Mr. Lewis," I say. "I'm Larry Noto with the Improv, here to pick you up."

Maybe he cracks a joke about not coming down, I forget. But he's coming – I *know* he is. The Hyatt has those silent glass elevators in the atrium. And sure enough, moments later I see this dark figure in a black beret descending like a comic god from above.

Like he's floating down from my dreams, into my real world.

We shake hands. He gets in my car – I'm driving a sharp-looking new Audi TT, which is what you can swing when you live rent-free at home with your parents. His eyes go wide.

"Oh, my God, look at this car!" he says. "We should jerk off and go to Paris!"

I don't even know what that means. But it sounds like the coolest thing.

Jerk off and go to Paris? Sure, let's do it! And when he finds out I'm a fellow comedian, not some flunky chauffer hired by the club, he seems delighted.

"Oh, we're brothers!" he says. "That's so great!"

Turns out Richard Lewis couldn't be nicer. And for the rest of the weekend, this becomes our routine: me driving him back and forth between sets, the two of us having great conversations about comedy and life and everything else.

"I know people think I'm a pain in the ass," he says of not hanging with the other comics between sets. "It's not that I'm rude. It's a concentration thing. I just don't like being distracted when I'm focusing on my act."

One time we're driving to the club and we pass a plaza with a large concrete triangle in the middle and a sculpture in front.

"What's that?" Richard asks.

That's the Holocaust Memorial, I say.

His eyes widen.

"Oh, that's nice!" he says, lapsing into vintage paranoid mode. "It's like: 'Welcome to Baltimore, Jewboy!'"

Twenty-five minutes later, he tells that joke on-stage. It kills. On the ride back to the hotel, we start talking about it, analyzing it.

Now I practically have to pinch myself. Here I'm not only being accepted by Richard and treated as his equal – I'm talking shop with him!

I'm getting a crash course in Fundamentals of Comedy 101: Why a Joke Works!

I even remember the first time I really made him laugh. I was telling him how I had recently worked with Brett Butler (from ABC's "Grace Under Fire") and how she had told me: "Say hello to Richard for me."

"Oh, she's great," he said, "but she's obsessed because I wrote a book and she didn't. I think she was too busy fucking a squid"

Fucking a squid? What did that even mean?

But without a pause or even fully knowing if it made sense, I said, "Well… it ran out of ink."

It was the "at bat" I had been training for my whole life. Richard looked at me like I had just crushed a grand slam. It remains a top moment in my life.

Well, the weekend just speeds by. After his last gig, Richard tells me I'm one of the nicest, most professional comics he's ever met.

"I didn't get to see a lot of your act," he says. "But you're funny. You're a natural. I can tell just by being with you the last few days. Keep writing, keep at it. Because I know our paths will cross again."

The whole wonderful weekend means so much to me.

Through hard work and perseverance and luck and moxie – *What?! You think you can stand up in front of 300 people and make 'em laugh, kid?*– my childhood dream had become reality.

More real than I could have ever imagined.

Here I had just shared the stage with one of the true gods of comedy. How many people get to do anything like that with their heroes?

Let's face it, you can be good at golf and never play with Tiger Woods. You can be great at baseball and never get to hang in the dugout with Cal Ripken, Jr.

I was getting to play the game I loved in one of the best facilities in the business with some of the greatest players in history.

I drove Richard Lewis in my car and it was glorious.

LARRY LIVE

Speed Dating

So I tried this speed-dating thing.

A company sets this up. The concept is that single people sign up to go on a series of eight-minute dates in the same room with a variety of people throughout the night.

It's one eight-minute date after another.

Over and over and over again.

But I actually met someone. We clicked. And we decided to go out on a real date the next night. And it was going GREAT!

We talked, we laughed, we shared stories about our families and our lives and our goals. Really connected.

Then the ninth minute of the date came. And I don't know . . . we just started drifting apart.

I could tell we were becoming different people . . .

And she got all needy and clingy. And I was like: "Look, if I wanted to spend 10 minutes with someone, I'd get married!"

CHAPTER 9

LEARNING AT THE FEET OF THE MASTERS

The Improv became my second home, not that I had any visions about quitting my day job. Actually, the two occupations could sometimes combine for bizarre effect.

One day when the marketing office for Harbor Magic was being relocated from the Pier 5 Hotel to the Admiral Fell Inn in Fells Point, I was outside the hotel lugging boxes and putting them in a van. I was in jeans and a grungy shirt, sweating my ass off, when I noticed a man nearby watching me.

This went on for several minutes, to the point where it got awkward.

Finally he said: "I'm sorry. I don't mean to stare. But aren't you a comedian?"

"Apparently not a very good one," I said with a laugh, grabbing another box.

On the other hand, at least no one had come up to me that day and said: "Hey, I don't mean to stare. But aren't you a *mover?*"

The truth was, I was getting better and better at standup, and more and more comfortable in front of all sorts of audiences. You couldn't help but get better at the craft just by observing all the brilliant comics passing through the Improv's doors.

One was Frank Caliendo, the terrific young comic making a name for himself with his dead-on impressions of NFL announcer John Madden and actor Morgan Freeman, among others.

I opened for Caliendo one Sunday night and did this joke about how sex was like miniature golf: there are some holes it's impossible to get into, holes where the windmill is just a tease, holes where . . . anyway, you get where this was going.

Nowhere.

I knew it wasn't a great routine. It was clunky and unpolished because I had never really done it before.

When my eight minutes were up, I went back-stage and immediately started to brood. I was upset because I thought the bit had potential and I had pretty much fucked it up.

When I got to the green room, Caliendo was lying down.

Quickly, he turned to me and said: "That's not you, with that routine. What are you *doing?* Please! Sex is like miniature golf? Sex is like driving a bus, sex is like a rotisserie chicken, sex is like . . .?"

He rolled his eyes. And I got it.

He wasn't trying to be mean. He was saying: It's been done! Sex is like . . . everyone's done sex-is-like stuff!

He had listened to my act and heard me do my jokes about growing up Italian, along with a new joke I was doing about TV commercials, in which I could get all worked up.

"You should do the jokes you're passionate about," Caliendo went on. "Like the TV ones and family ones. That stuff."

Jay Moher, who was incredibly pompous, was another comic who taught me a lesson – albeit a harsh one – about the business.

Back-stage one night, I happened to tell him that people often mistook me for Dan Snyder, the owner of the Washington Redskins. (I *do* bear a strong facial resemblance to Snyder, although my bank account – I know this will shock you – bears absolutely no resemblance to his.)

Anyway, I told Mohr: "I get 'Hey, are you Dan Snyder?'" all the time at bars, restaurants, concerts, etc.

"I even got it at lunch the other day," I continued. "I felt like saying: "Yeah, I'm Dan Snyder, the billionaire. That's why I'm having lunch at a Chili's in Bel Air on a Saturday afternoon."

Well, Mohr thought this was hysterical.

When he picked himself off the floor and stopped laughing, he said: "That's so funny! You gotta open with that!"

I wasn't so sure.

This is Baltimore, I told him. They might not even know who Dan Snyder is. Plus, I don't want to go out there and start with a joke I've never told before.

Mohr snorted derisively.

"What?" he said, gesturing toward the audience. "You think they're here to see *you*? They don't care about *you*!"

The remark hurt. At the time, I thought: what a jerk.

But his point was: what the fuck difference does it make? Go out and bomb! They don't give a shit if you bomb. They're only here to see me. What, you think they're gonna walk out of here tonight and go: "God, the opener's first joke was awful?!"

In the end, I didn't do it.

I just couldn't open with an unknown joke. I took my emceeing job seriously. I was the face of the club, in a way, the host, the guy who first welcomed you after you sat down and ordered drinks.

I wanted to come out strong, with material that was time-tested. I didn't want to stumble over a new joke I was still sorting out in my head.

Louie Anderson, Brett Butler, Bill Burr – all of them were generous with their praise and advice for a fledgling comic still trying to find his way.

I was making Anderson laugh in the green room between shows one night and he said: "You're funny on stage, but you're even funnier in here. Whatever *this* is, will make you a great comic."

It was big advice. Be myself.

The thing I remember about Bill Burr was that he was so gifted and talented – at a level most of us comics would have *killed* to be at. Yet he was struggling over the fact that he wasn't getting to the next level, whatever that would be.

He talked about it in the green room. He talked about having done Comedy Central and Dave Chappelle's show, but not having a sitcom and not having appeared in any movies. You could read the disappointment on his face.

He wasn't taking the next step up the comedy-success ladder. And there's always a next step. Listening to him, I thought: *Man, this is a never-ending quest, stardom. Or whatever it is we're all chasing here.*

Sometimes, the headliner and the other comedian on the show that weekend would just hang out and have fun, especially if they developed a good rapport during the gigs.

The late Robert Schimmel (from "The Howard Stern Show" fame) took me to dinner at the Prime Rib, one of the most upscale steakhouses in Baltimore. And in between efficient waiters in tuxedos silently bringing items to the table, he would tell me some of the dirtiest stories and jokes I'd ever heard, full of lascivious hook-ups and three-somes and other sexual adventures I could barely comprehend.

Ralphie May from "Last Comic Standing" and I decided to go see the last new "Star Wars" movie together at the historic Senator Theatre. Ralphie is a *big* guy. *BIG*. When I pulled up in my little Audi TT, he screamed "HELL NO!" and hopped in a cab.

Bob Saget was absolutely filthy – on- and off-stage. Let's get that out of the way first.

He's known for hosting "America's Funniest Home Videos" and for playing Danny Tanner, the quirky, unhip, dad of three adorable daughters on the sitcom "Full House" that ran from 1987-1995.

But let me tell you something: of all the comedians I've worked with, none ever got more female attention than Bob Saget.

I remember taking him after one show to a place called Babalu

Grill near the Improv. It was late and I mentioned that the bars in Baltimore closed at 2.

"I'm Bob Saget," he said. "They'll stay open."

I know it sounds arrogant, but it didn't come off that way. It came off simply as him stating a fact.

Sure enough, the bar stayed open. And the women flocked to him. We sat at a table having drinks and smoking cigars, with a red velvet rope separating our VIP section from the riff-raff.

And a steady parade of women came up to talk to him. See, they were all in love with Danny Tanner way back when. Now here he was – well, a slightly older version, anyway – right here in their midst all these years later!

They were all going ga-ga, wanting to tell him how great he was and much he meant to their dreamy adolescent lives! And meanwhile, Mr. Saget, I can assure you, was not fantasizing about helping them out with their homework.

He didn't take anyone back to his hotel that night. But he'd definitely had a few drinks. At one point on the ride back, watching the bars empty and the crowds spilling onto the streets, he snarled: "Look at all these people! I hate these people! I hope they all get SARS!"

It was funny and sick and completely over the top. And I kept thinking: *What is wrong with you?* even as I laughed.

Back at the hotel, though, Bob told me that he'd had fun. And he encouraged me to keep at it, keep working on my act.

"I'm positive our paths will cross again," he said.

Unfortunately, while we traded a few emails, we never again worked together.

Instead, the next "name" comedian to cross my path was a short guy in an Italian leather jacket.

And he *definitely* didn't have my best interests at heart.

LARRY LIVE

Being Catholic

I'm Italian and therefore Catholic. 'Cause that's the law.

We're not hard-core Catholics, though. We only go to Mass on Easter and Christmas – because I guess that's the absolute minimum requirement for getting into heaven.

I hate going on those days because it's so crowded. Because that's when all the other part-time Catholics show up.

You can't even get seats in the main church. It's like a sold-out concert you can't get tickets to.

Altar boys are out in the parking lot scalping seats:

"Anybody need a pew? C'mon, who needs a pew? I got pews here! Good seats, too. Right by the altar . . ."

So you have to go to the back-up Mass. That's the Mass they have in the school gym/cafeteria.

They're putting the psalms up on the scoreboard . . .

And you know you're getting screwed, because in the main church they have an opera singer and a full orchestra.

And at the back-up Mass, we have a fucking eight-year-old on a Casio keyboard. And a grandmother with a tambourine.

Lent is a fascinating time for me, too.

Now, not all of you are Catholic. So for the sinners that are going to burn in hell, let me explain.

Lent is the time of year when we as Catholics show our love for the Lord by not eating meat on Fridays.

He sacrificed for us, the thinking goes. So we're going to sacrifice for Him.

But let's look at this trade, OK?

HIS sacrifice was that He died while nailed to a cross.

Our sacrifice? No Big Mac today.

And of course my family would show their sacrifice by going to Red Lobster and eating as much seafood as humanly possible.

We'd order:

"I'll have the shrimp . . ."

"I'll have the scallops . . ."

"The lobster for me, please . . ."

But if the waitress asked: "Would you like to add a steak to that?" we'd all look horrified.

"Oh, no!" we'd shout. "Hey, we love Jesus!"

AND NOW...

AN ALBUM

Me around 4 years old. Notice that "All in the Family" is on the television. TV shows were a big part of my childhood. No wonder I'm dressed like Isaac the bartender in "The Love Boat."

My Dad, sister, my grandparents and I waiting for the Main Street Electrical Parade at the Magic Kingdom in Walt Disney World in 1986. Walt once said, "It all started with a mouse." Well, as for my Disney addiction, it all started with this trip. Must have been the hat.

My mom and I at Fenway Park to see the Orioles take on the Red Sox. She raised me a die-hard Baltimore sports fan.

Me as Cornelius Hackl in John Carroll's production of "Hello, Dolly!" This is how all the girls in high school looked at me. Once again, must have been the hat.

Interviewing Barry "Greg Brady" Williams during "The Larry Noto Show One Year Birthday Bash" in front of a 600-person crowd at Loyola University. Apparently, Gilligan wasn't available.

The first segment I produced for the "Rodricks for Breakfast" show was nominated for a regional Emmy. Our local newspaper, The Aegis, played it up big.

My good friend and comedy supporter, Tracey Harrington McCoy, was my guest at the Emmy ceremonies. This is not my Emmy and she is not my girlfriend – but at least I have this photo. It was an honor just to be nominated.

The first time I ever did stand-up comedy was at an open mic night at Winchester's Comedy Club on Water Street in Baltimore, in 1994.

The club I perform the most at the most these days, and the first major club I headlined, is Magooby's Joke House in Timonium, Maryland.

One of my most memorable gigs at the Baltimore Comedy Factory had a group of 100 deaf patrons in the audience. A sign language interpreter was on the stage with me during my set. She got bigger laughs than I did.

My first weekend gig at the Baltimore Improv with the great Brian Regan and Bob Somerby. I was lucky to work with masters of their craft from the very beginning.

Dom Irrera and I first worked together when I was starting out as a comedian at the Baltimore Improv.

We'd be reunited years later for a gig at Magooby's Joke House but he was too busy to look up from his phone to take a picture with me. Show business changes people.

Louie Anderson helped me channel some of my confidence behind the scenes and be more myself on stage.

Rams Head On Stage in Annapolis has been good to me over the years. I've worked with legends such as Robert Klein (above) and Brad Garrett (below).

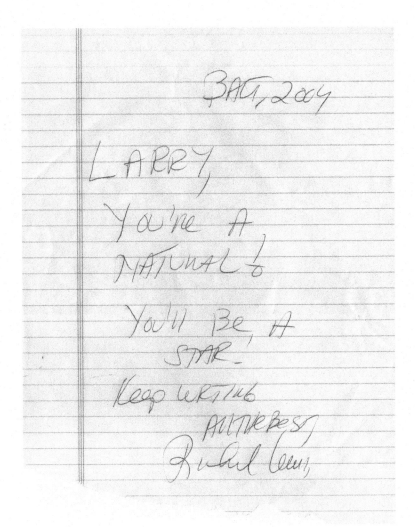

This letter from Richard Lewis hangs in my office at home.

Visit Baltimore sponsored the gift bags for the Broadway premier of "Hairspray," based on Charm City native John Waters' classic film. I got to attend the star-studded after-party and became best friends with people like Martin Short.

Dom DeLuise and I at the National Italian American Foundation Gala in DC. Dom was always one of my favorites, especially in Mel Brooks' "History of the World: Part One."

I kept running into him and finally gave him my Loyola Student Government Association business card. Days later I received this autographed postcard with a joking reference to our multiple meetings.

On stage at Brad Garrett's Comedy Club on the Las Vegas Strip. I was curious how I would do outside of the East Coast. Turns out even people from Iowa thought I was funny.

I made it! My name is on a lobby sign at Brad Garrett's Comedy Club! Sure, Gladys Knight had her own marquee, but still... The club had the sign shipped to me and it now proudly hangs in my house (my sign, not Gladys').

Orioles manager Buck Showalter with our "In Buck We Trust" shirt at Orioles FanFest. He thought he was signing the shirt but was actually signing an image release form.

"In Buck We Trust" was sold in major sports stores throughout the Baltimore region, including the Sports Legends Museum store at Oriole Park at Camden Yards.

No Wife. No Kids. No Wonder.

The Christmas card I sent out featuring me and my family... The Muppets. Some people thought this was taken at Disney or the Henson studios in California. But it's my basement. Explains a lot.

Artwork by the talented cartoonist Garth Gerhart for our Dos Equis spoof, The Most Interesting Elf in the World.

Me and the kids at Anne Stewart Pershall's class at St. John the Evangelist school in Severna park talking Orioles, John Denver, and The Muppets.

The "Let's Go O's" song and ensuing publicity reunited me with Sister Marie Gregory, the woman who helped start it all in my high school days. Sister Marie introduced me to everyone she could with her infamous joke, "This boy was a pain in my back pew."

Keeping my dad's legacy alive at Music Land in Bel Air, Maryland. Every morning when I open the store, I declare "Welcome to the land of music!" and then sing like Gene Wilder. I think the team likes it.

CHAPTER 10

"I'M GONNA HELP YOU OUT"

Vinnie Favorito blew into town like a dark summer squall.

He was this insult comic from Boston who favored slick-back hair, shades and black leather jackets.

Most of his act consisted of taking shots at various audience members in the vein of a junior varsity Don Rickles.

People thought it was off the cuff – and to some degree it was.

But it was also formulaic: find the fat guy in the audience. Find the black guy. Find the Mexican. Find the Jew. Find the dumb broad.

Then go to town on them.

Dump all over them with an often-venomous mixture of sexist, racist, ethnic and anti-Semitic jokes. Then hope a few of the hyenas in the crowd – at least the ones with three or four Budweisers floating in their guts – get to chortling, which might offset the strained nervous laughter coming from lots of other folks.

Not that Vinnie F. wasn't funny – even wildly inventive at times.

"Racism exists in this country, and I'm sick of it," went one of my favorite bits of his. "But I think the real problem is the slang (words) that we have for each other. Like me, I'm Italian, so they'll call me a guinea or a dago or a wop. Mexicans, what do they call you? Beaner or wetback. Asian people, they call you gook or chink.

"And black people, we call you . . ." – here he puts his hand over his mouth and semi-mumbles, "you know, black people."

The audience howled.

Which he followed by saying: "Did you see the white people? They're like" – here he widened his eyes in feigned terror – "where's he going with this?"

I opened for Vinnie all weekend and he was super-nice to me. One night after the show, we ended up having dinner at Sabatino's in Little Italy. (Hey, it's one of the few places that serves food till 3 a.m.!)

"Listen, I really think you're great," he said to me at one point. "I think you're *so* funny. And I'm gonna help you out."

Maybe my internal sonar should have been pinging at this point. *Warning: con man closing in fast!*

But – as usual – it didn't.

There's no doubt about it: I had a serial case of naiveté back then – even after my experience with the unsavory R.G. years earlier.

Even Vinnie's next remark failed to make me suspicious.

"What I want you to do," he continued, "is write out all your jokes and mail them to me. And I'll help you punch them up."

He proceeded to tell me that he would help me get gigs and that Budd Friedman, the legendary founder of the Improv comedy clubs, was a personal friend.

When I mentioned having worked with Dom Irrera, Vinnie said Dom was a great friend of his, too.

"Just send me the jokes," Vinnie said again, "and I'll help you write them and get some gigs."

On the drive back to his hotel, Vinnie grilled me about my family and what my folks did for a living. I had borrowed my dad's car, a shiny black Jeep Grand Cherokee, which seemed to impress Vinnie to no end.

"Oh, nice car!" he gushed. "So your dad, he does well?"

I told him the story of how my dad had built up his music store from scratch, growing the business year after year until it had become a successful and beloved institution in Harford County.

Vinnie seemed absolutely riveted.

When I finally dropped him off, he said, "Let's stay in touch." And he urged me again to send him my jokes.

I never did send the jokes. For the first time, I was mildly suspicious of Mr. Favorito. Especially after a friend advised that if I mailed Vinnie the jokes, he could legally claim they were now his property and refuse to give them back.

But Vinnie F. wasn't through with me just yet.

A few weeks later, while at a business dinner for Harbor Magic at a Baltimore restaurant, I checked my phone and discovered a voice-mail.

"Hey, Larry, it's Vinnie," the message said. "How you doing? I'm working on this game show, an Italian game show and Dom's doing it, too. He's gonna play the judge, and we have a part I think you'd be great for. Give me a call."

I went back to my dinner. But inside I was ready to explode.

This is big! I kept thinking. *This is what I've been waiting for! This is my big break!*

(I know, I know . . . I was back to being terminally gullible. What can I say? Guilty as charged.)

I called Vinnie back as soon as I could.

He seemed all revved up about the new game show.

"What I need to know," he said, "is how flexible are you with your job? If I need you to get on a plane and fly to L.A. the next day – 'cause this is really gonna be great! – could you do that?"

I was so excited I could barely get the words out.

Yeah, I said. I'd have to talk to my boss and get approval. But, sure, I can get out to L.A.!

"Great," Vinnie said.

We talked for a few more minutes and he promised to get back to me.

About a week later, my cell phone rang around midnight. I was still living with my parents, so I grabbed the phone quickly so the noise wouldn't wake them.

It was Vinnie calling from Las Vegas.

After some more small talk about the terrific new game show we were to be part of, Vinnie got down to business.

"Listen," he said, "I did for you. And now I need you to do for me. I'm doing this comedy album, OK? But I need to front the money to the guy who's producing it. I don't have it right now. But if you help me, you'd be like an official backer. So you'd get your money back, plus another 50 per cent."

There was a pause.

The he honed in for the kill.

"Can you Western Union me $5,000 tonight?" he asked.

Excuse me?

I was so stunned I didn't answer at first.

Here I was, still living at home, with my day job and some gigs at the Improv that were loads of fun, but weren't exactly paying a lot.

And here was some guy twice my age, who I barely knew, asking me to send him five grand.

Tonight.

Via Western Union.

"Vinnie," I finally stammered, "I'd have to talk to my lawyer and my accountant . . ."

"What lawyers?" Vinnie said. "*Lawyers*? I thought we were friends! I thought we were pals! We don't need lawyers!"

And that was finally when it hit me.

You know that scene at the end of "The Usual Suspects?" Where Chazz Palminteri, playing the customs cop, drops the coffee cup as he stares at a bulletin board? Because he sees that Verbal Kint, the gimp played by Kevin Spacey, has been feeding him a bullshit story all along?

And he suddenly realizes he's been played?

That's how it was with me.

Now it all made sense: Vinnie befriending me, promising gigs, asking about my folks, teasing me with a trumped-up new game show . . . the man was conning me big-time.

Vinnie was the Keyser Soze of comedy!

In that instant, I finally wised up. Hey, I may be gullible. But I'm not an idiot, OK?

In the end, I told Vinnie I just didn't have the money. And that was pretty much the last time I talked to him.

When I told some people at the Improv about Vinnie hitting me up for cash, they said he was famous for doing that. The word was that he had a heavy gambling problem.

Oh, I know this will shock you, too: I never heard another word about a new game show starring Vinnie Favorito.

Years later, I sent him a Facebook message to find out how he was doing. But he never responded.

And here's a sad post-script: in April of 2015, Vinnie's comedy show at the Flamingo Hotel in Las Vegas closed suddenly after 10 years.

According to a story in the *Las Vegas Review-Journal,* the closing followed "an employee's complaint related to a history of litigation involving personal loans."

The article went on to say that the employee had received a court judgment confirming that Favorito owed her $7,567. And it said a number of other people, including a personal injury attorney, Vinnie's ex-wife and a neighbor of his, were also owed substantial sums of money.

Understand, it gave me no great pleasure to read this. But once again, it all made sense.

In some respects, it would be the insult comic's final insult.

LARRY LIVE

Random Thoughts

I was talking with this attractive girl who works at the Disney Store. She's married, so it was just innocent flirting. We were bonding over our Disney addictions. She told me she had Disney tattoos. A Mickey on her ankle (which she showed me), a Belle rose on her ribs, and a Simba on her side.

I said: "I have one that says 'Supercalifragilisticexpialidocious,' but I shouldn't say where."

She high-fived me.

***

The dude in front of me at Target tonight was buying two 25-lb dumbbells. I was buying a Christmas cat toy for a cat that's not even mine. The little dividing bar on the belt represented the difference between the shit you buy when you're trying to get a girlfriend and the shit you buy when you have one.

***

I decided to do a 30-day Ab Challenge. After six days, it won. Now the app icon on my iPhone has changed from a stick figure doing sit-ups to a fat guy watching TV.

It's gone from challenging me to mocking me.

***

I thought my girlfriend being a nurse practitioner would add some spice to our personal life.

One night, I asked if I could be her "patient." I ended up on two new meds and a low salt diet.

***

If I were Amanda Knox, I wouldn't even go to the Olive Garden.

***

On the drive up to Atlantic City, my dad put on his headphones and listened to his iPod for the entire drive. It was like traveling with a teenager who was too cool to engage in conversation. The only difference being that the music coming out of the headphones was accordion polkas.

***

Chick-fil-A just announced: "NEW COW CALENDARS NOW AVAILABLE!"

Dear Santa . . .

CHAPTER 11

"THE NIGHT THE LAUGHTER DIED"

The Improv continued to feel like my own personal comedy school, featuring a steady parade of big name talent that I could study and learn from.

Like any cross-section of humanity, some of these big names were good people. And others were – to use the technical term – assholes.

The biggest asshole of all might have been Dustin Diamond.

Diamond, you may recall, played dorky goofball Screech on "Saved by the Bell," the popular sitcom about six high school friends that ran from the late 80's to the early 90's.

And on the weekend that the Improv gave me my first feature slot – the comic who goes on second, right before the headliner -- they had booked Diamond to be the big name.

Maybe it was all those years playing a hopeless nerd that made him seem like a guy trying *way* too hard to be cool – not to mention a guy who was *way* too full of himself.

In any event, upon arriving in Baltimore, Diamond decided that he didn't want anyone else sharing the green room with him.

This edict was conveyed in no uncertain terms to the other comics by Diamond's manager, who was also his girlfriend. She also listed all the topics we were to avoid in our routines that could possibly conflict with Dustin's material.

Including, she said, "grandma porn."

Huh?

Grandma porn?

"Oh, well, there goes my first 10 minutes!" I said sarcastically. "No grandma porn jokes? You're killing me here."

Since we weren't allowed in the green room, I had to sit on a stool next to the DJ booth on my first night as a feature. Here I had shared the green room with a host of comedy legends and finally worked my way up – at least for the weekend – from being the opening act.

And fucking Screech, of all people, was making me cool my heels between sets next to the heavily tatted guy with the backward baseball cap who was pumping music!

Yeah. That put me in a great mood.

To make things even worse, Diamond's act was just awful, with the bit about grandma porn being about as funny as you'd imagine it would be.

Topping it all off, he had brought along a Polaroid camera for anyone who wanted a photo taken with him – for which, naturally, he charged $10.

Oh, Diamond was a sweetheart, all right. Everyone who worked in the club was in agreement: if we could have lured him up to the roof and pushed him off, we would have.

Not long after his Improv gig, Diamond went on to "star" in an embarrassing sex tape with the classy title of "Screeched: Saved by the Smell." (He later insisted his role had been handled by a "stunt double.").

And in 2014, Diamond famously made headlines when he was sentenced to four months in jail for his involvement in a Christmas Day barroom brawl in which he allegedly pulled a switchblade knife and stabbed someone.

Yep, a class act if ever there was one.

Angry rant-master Lewis Black, on the other hand, was a fascinating character to be around.

People always want to know if comedians are the same in real life as they appear to be on stage.

Is it just an act they're doing for the audience?

Or are they really as enraged or spaced out or neurotic or psychotic as they appear to be?

All I know is, the first time I worked with Lewis Black, he erupted like a volcano right in front of my eyes.

I walked into the green room and found him standing in front of the TV, screaming "AARRGGHH! FUCK YOU!" at it while giving it the finger – with *both* middle fingers!

I don't remember what he was watching. But the veins in his neck were standing up and he looked as if he was about to have a coronary.

So I said to myself: "Ohhh-kay. Guess with ol' Lew Black, it's not an act."

But Black, for all his wild-eyed, arm-waving bluster, also seemed to be amazed – and appreciative – of his lot in life.

He was already a big star because of his frequent appearances on Comedy Central's "The Daily Show." But right before he took the Improv stage one night, I witnessed a brief exchange between Lewis and a long-time friend that proved revealing.

The place was packed that night and the two of them were listening to the buzz of anticipation in the room in the moments before Black would be introduced.

"I know, can you fucking *believe* this?!" Black said to his buddy as they looked out at the audience.

Like: *They're here to see me, dude! Look how far I've come!*

You could tell he was still in awe of – and still got a kick from – his ability to sell out a comedy club. It was really a neat moment to see.

But for me, the world came crashing down on a hot August weekend in 2005.

No major headliner had been booked at the Improv that weekend, which was odd. It was just three local comics – me, Doug Powell and Erik Myers – on the bill. I was scheduled to open for Richard Lewis the following weekend. But word had spread quickly that both of the Improv managers were leaving and rumors were flying everywhere.

I started to get a bad vibe. Then I wondered if I wasn't over-reacting.

The president of the Improv was there that evening. Maybe, we thought, this has something to do with the change in managers. And there were a group of men in the audience who were obviously affiliated with the club in some capacity.

"Maybe they're scouts from the other Improvs," another comic said hopefully. "Maybe they're here 'cause we're all local. And we're all gonna get gigs out of this."

Anyway, I emceed the show and all went well. When it was over, I took the mic and said: "Hope you had a great time! We're here all weekend, tell your friends! I'll be here next weekend with Richard Lewis. Come back and see us! Have a great night! Good-bye everybody!"

On my way out, I waved to the Improv president and said: "See you tomorrow night!"

He waved back. Then he said: "Actually, Larry, wait up a sec . . ."

Uh-oh.

A moment later, I saw Al, one of the managers who was leaving, with a bunch of folded checks in his hand.

And that's when I knew.

"It's all over," I whispered to Erik Myers.

And it was.

In short order, the Improv president gave us the bad news. The club was closing.

Those guys in the audience who seemed to be Improv people? They were actually movers, with trucks parked out back. Now they were taking everything out of the place, furniture, wall decorations, booze, food, kitchen utensils, you name it – and stripping the place bare.

It reminded me of the horrible winter night in 1983 when the Baltimore Colts slipped out of town bound for Indianapolis, all their stuff packed away in Mayflower vans.

The ostensible reason for the Improv's closing, the *Sun* reported, was "rowdy conditions at Power Plant Live!" that "made it impossible to continue doing business there."

A club spokeswoman added that customers had complained about having to walk through young, drunken revelers to get to the shows. And that music from the concert venue next door bled through the walls, distracting the comedians.

But those weren't the real reasons.

"It wasn't profitable, that's what (management) said," I told a *Sun* reporter. And that seemed closer to the truth than anything else.

Whatever the reason for the closing, I was devastated. I'm not ashamed to say that I went around the corner that night and broke down sobbing.

I couldn't stop thinking: there goes Richard Lewis, there goes my club, there goes my home.

For so many of us, the Improv was where we had honed our comedy chops, developed our sense of self-worth in a business that could take a machete to your ego at any moment. The closing was sad for the city, too. Now there was no place where people could go to see A-list comedians like Kevin Pollack and Louis Anderson, Lewis Black, Dave Chappelle and the great Richard Lewis anymore.

For me, I had lost my stage. I'd had the two greatest years of my life appearing at the Improv. It had been everything I'd dreamt about since I was a kid. And it had all come crashing down with no warning.

Not long after, I wrote a short piece for *Baltimore* magazine about how wounded I felt over the club's closing. They titled it "The Night the Laughter Died." Maybe that strikes you as melodramatic. But for me, it was perfect.

"Where am I supposed to try out new jokes now?" I wrote. "At my day job? In the middle of a meeting? 'Yes, I think those numbers speak for themselves. By the way, what's up with these commercials for milk and cheese? Are there really people out there who haven't heard of these things yet?'"

I wouldn't get over that horrible night for a long, long time.

LARRY LIVE

Wild World of Sports

The Olympics have taught me to hate countries I either never thought about or never even knew existed.

Like Canada.

I never think about Canada. I have no ill will towards Canada.

Until the Winter Olympics.

Until Canada played the U.S. for the gold medal in hockey. And about 30 seconds into this thing, I HATED CANADA SO MUCH!

And then they beat us. And I was like: "FUCK CANADA!"

What is that, maple syrup?! Get that shit out of this house!

And is that a John Candy movie? Turn that crap off, too!

And some of these countries really go to extremes to win, don't they? Like changing genders to compete.

Look, I don't work out because I don't like to change CLOTHES, ok? And these athletes are changing their SEX!

There was a controversy once where a "female" won the gold medal. And then the committee said they might have to take the medal away because they weren't sure if it was a man or a woman.

So they had to do a gender test . . .

And the list of things they were going to do to her! Like an MRI, a CAT scan, blood work . . .

Um, how about a set of eyes on her? Wouldn't that work?

Or how about a hand?

Look, I'm lonely. Put ME on the committee. I'll figure her gender out real fast.

And here's the kicker: it was going to take six weeks to get the results.

SIX WEEKS?!

You know what? If you can hide your balls for six weeks... hell, you get to keep your medal!

CHAPTER 12

THE GREAT ESCAPE

I have a joke in my act where I tell people that I lived at home with my parents for a long time.

A long, long time.

Even though my dad made the immigrant journey from Italy, a mover he was not. I believed he landed on U.S. soil, put his stuff down and said: "That's it. We're not going anywhere else."

My parents lived in an apartment, a townhouse and a single home – all within one mile of his business. I was convinced my dad's car was actually on one of those rails you see on the antique car ride at amusement parks – it only went between home and work.

So when I started getting to the point of needing to move out, my parents kept enticing me to stay.

They offered: an addition with my own bedroom!

My own bathroom!

Meals included! Served by showgirls!

But, alas, at age 30, it was time to go. When I told them the news, they wept and wore black for a month.

The truth was, I hadn't really minded living at home. I worked, I had events, I was constantly busy. And whether I got home at 9 at night or 1 in the morning, there was food in the house. And I wasn't paying for anything, either.

On the other hand, you do get a lot of shit from people when they hear you're still living at home in your 30's. And it's hard to bring women home. On the rare occasions that I did, it was always awkward at breakfast the next morning.

My mom would be puttering around the kitchen, only to stick her head out and inquire: "Does the whore want some French toast?"

I was appalled!

"Come on, mom," I'd tell her. "You *know* she likes pancakes."

OK, that never really happened. Are you kidding? If I'd brought a woman home to spend the night, my parents' heads would have exploded.

But when it finally came time to move out, my parents came up with a different way to keep me close by.

"There's a house across the street for sale," they said.

"Look," I said, "this isn't 'Everybody Loves Raymond.' When I move out, there will be a vehicle involved."

Plus I had this image of my mother carrying a tray of lasagna, with our little dog trailing her, down the court to my house.

So late in 2006, I moved instead into a townhouse eight miles away. Naturally, my parents acted like I'd moved to Istanbul.

The saving grace is that my mother is actually an amazing interior decorator. She doesn't do it for a living, but she has tremendous taste. So now she had another house to furnish.

When my mom walked into an Ethan Allen showroom, it was like Norm walking into Cheers. They celebrated, they cheered. The sales people would have little tears of joy running down their cheeks. They knew it was going to be a good day.

We were so close to the sales woman at Ethan Allen that when I had my walk-through at the new townhouse, she came with us to measure for the window treatments. And my mom would just randomly buy shit to bring to my house.

So now I was like Dick Van Dyke nearly tripping over an ottoman in the living room that I didn't have the day before. I was standing in the kitchen one afternoon, opening the mail, when I noticed a gravy boat on the top shelf.

A gravy boat that hadn't been there earlier that morning.

First of all, I'm 30 years old and single. I don't have a lot of people over for gravy, OK? I'm not going out to the clubs and asking people: "Want to come over to my place for some bangers and mash?"

Then my mom bought me a KitchenAid mixer. It's still never been used.

Apparently I was gonna bring women over and they would be impressed with this 'cause it's a status symbol. I guess it's not a bad thing if a woman wants to date me just because of my mixer. At least I'd get baked goods out of the deal.

The kitchen was like a prop on a movie set. It was full of things that had never been used.

When you're buying a new house, you go over the options with the builders. They said: "Do you want a gas range? Or an electric range?"

I said: "What's a range? What I want is a little Italian lady to cook for me."

This was my mother's greatest concern: How would I eat living alone? I'd always had a home-cooked meal waiting for me. What would I do now?

Living alone. In the wilderness.

So my mom would ask me to come over for dinner, which I often did. We'd watch "Lost" together. Or an Orioles game.

But life gets busy. It became harder and harder to get over there for dinner. But . . . YOU HAVE TO EAT!

So now I would meet my mother in a parking lot. I'd be sitting in my car when suddenly the grey Volvo SUV would show up, approaching from the opposite direction.

Slowly it would pull up next to me.

An arm would extend out the window. The arm would be holding a large bag filled with . . . a plastic container of pasta.

It was like an Italian mother drive-by.

Before I moved out, the joke was: who was my neighbor going to be? This was key, apparently. My friends were always telling me: "Oh, you gotta get a house! You gotta get a mortgage! You'll have sex all the time!"

Well, I got a house. And I got a mortgage. But I sure wasn't seeing a return on my investment in the other department.

It didn't take long to see why.

LARRY LIVE

Dating

Trying to get married at my age is like trying to sell a house in a bad economy. Maybe you can do it. But you know you would have done better 10 years earlier.

I also know that I'm the house that's been on the market forever. People drive by and shake their heads and go: "Boy, they just can't move that thing . . ."

It's hard to be optimistic about marriage the older you get. Because you've been through it all. You've seen how it ends.

Dating at my age is like watching the movie "Titanic" and trying to convince yourself that it ends differently this time.

Like the movie, it's always great in the beginning.

Everyone's having a good time . . . there's music and dancing . . . a few steamy windows . . .

But in the end, you know that ship's going down.

There's an iceberg out there somewhere . . .

Usually it presents itself early on. But we're so excited that someone might be even remotely interested in us that we just keep sailing on.

I was on a date with a girl who said she didn't watch "The Office" until AFTER Steve Carrell left the show. And I told myself: "Just look at her boobs. Just look at her boobs . . ."

I was with another girl who said she didn't like the movie "Old School."

Now, it's not THAT she didn't like the movie, it's WHY she didn't like it. I asked her to explain.

"I don't know," she said. "He was older but was still in school. I couldn't follow it."

OH . . . MY . . . GOD!

You can't follow "Old School?" You got lost in the plot?

I guess we're not going to discuss "Inception" tonight, are we?

On a related note, I have this tremendous track record where every girl I've gone out with has gotten married to the very next guy they've gone out with.

The very next guy . . . and – BOOM! – just like that they're married. I guess he's so fantastic in comparison to me that they snatch him up.

So I'm going to start my own dating service.

If there are any single, beautiful women out there looking for the man of your dreams, you need to go out with me.

I won't be him – but I'll guarantee you that the NEXT guy will be.

I'm not Mr. Right.

I'm Mr. Right BEFORE Mr. Right.

CHAPTER 13

MEET THE NEIGHBORS

Whenever you move into a new house, you're always curious about your new neighbors.

I thought I would be having this revolving door of sex that my friends had told me about. On my first day in the new digs, I heard noises outside.

I peeked through the blinds.

My fantasy was to see a super-model in a bikini lying on a chaise lounge, the hot sun glistening on her body as golden droplets of water from the sprinkler slowly eased down her inner thigh.

Instead, there was this gray-haired 65-year-old woman pushing a lawn mower.

Wait, it gets better . . .

Turned out she was also a nun.

Her name was Nelda. And in the house cattycorner to her lived her good friend, Eileen, who was about 60.

Who had *also* been a nun before she left the order.

And both of them, I would discover, were psychoanalysts.

Nuns and analysts . . . they would judge me from every possible angle!

Long story short, I befriended them one day when I was putting up Christmas lights. Eileen stopped by to tell me how much she loved the holiday, because it reminded her of her dad, who had also been nuts about Christmas.

You should come over one night, I told Nelda and Eileen. So the first wild party I had in my new digs was with a couple of nuns.

I had never entertained on my own before. So I went to the supermarket and bought enough food to feed, I don't know, 30 nuns.

Wait a minute, I thought. Don't nuns take a vow of poverty? I could have a few hosts and some wine and they'd probably be set.

Instead, I bought so much cheese, crackers and fruit that when they walked in, they asked: "Who else is coming?"

It must have seemed like the entire Ravens team was stopping by.

But we had a great time together. I gave them a tour of the house. You'd think that would only take a few minutes. But it took about an hour and a half. We'd look at a photo of Frank Sinatra, for example, and then we'd have a spirited 15-minute conversation about Ol' Blue Eyes.

After the tour we had a wonderful talk about life and energy, and the meaning of existence and one's purpose here on Earth.

"Your lights, your Christmas trees, it's all a celebration of joy," Nelda and Eileen informed me.

We talked about bright lights and dark lights, and that there was a reason I had bought that house. It was really like having a guardian angel next to me, on both sides of the couch.

Anyway, we talked and talked and finally my house phone rang. But I didn't answer it – just kept talking. Then my cell phone rang. And it was in the kitchen. So I excused myself and went to answer it.

At that point, I figured it was around, oh, 10 at night. Instead, I looked at the clock and it was quarter to one in the morning. And it was my mother calling on my cell.

"Why didn't you call to tell me how it went?" she asked. My silence triggered her next question. "Are the nuns still there!?"

The next day at work, I was exhausted. And I had to tell everyone:

"Well, I was partying hard with the nuns last night . . ."

But a true friendship was formed. You wouldn't normally call a 60-ish nun and ex-nun your best friends. But it was very clear we were connected. It was clear we were meant to meet. And from then on, they've played very important roles in my life.

They've been through all my breakups with girlfriends, all my struggles at work. They've talked to me about my life purpose, that if it's to bring joy to the world through comedy or radio or TV shows, then I need to stay true to that. And if it's being close to my family and friends and by going to Disney World and by putting up more Christmas decorations than Clark Griswald, then I need to stay true to that too.

Of course, it becomes increasingly difficult as life goes on to keep that perspective. Rejection, jobs that fail, relationships that go south, projects that don't work out, encounters with more and more assholes – all of it can wear you down.

It's very easy, Nelda and Eileen reminded me, for the darkness to win.

We grew so close, the three of us, that I even gave them the keys to my house. My friends were incredulous over this.

But I said: "Look, you can trust a nun. 'Cause if a nun steals from you, you should just kill yourself. That's the burning bush right there.

"I'm sorry, if you walk into your house and your DVD player's missing and you're like 'Damn it! Sister Mary Margaret did this!' that's God giving you the middle finger. That's Him saying: 'I don't give a fuck about you!'"

On one memorable occasion, Nelda put her arm around me and said: "Oh, God, if I was 30 years younger . . ."

"Yeah, and not married to Jesus," I said. "Let's not forget about that."

That would be a tough act to follow in the dating world, wouldn't it? Following God in a relationship?

I could see the conversation:

Me: "Oh, so what did your ex do?"

Nelda: "Well, He created the world. He was so full of Himself. He had a Him complex. And what do *you* do?"

Me: "Oh, I'm a comedian . . ."

I mean, you can't follow an act like God's!

We've had a lot of laughs over the years, though. It's been like a sitcom. One year, I fell off a ladder and nearly broke my ankle. Nelda and Eileen saw my mom trying to get me into the car. They ran out, helped her and jumped in the car to take me to the emergency room. As they walked me in the ER, one of them under each shoulder – the way an NFL player is taken off the field – a nurse asked "Are these your grandmothers?"

Even though I was in extreme pain, I knew the set up. I paused, looked up and said: "No, these are my nuns. They go everywhere with me."

Our friendship taught me: surround yourself with good people. Surround yourself with bright lights.

You'll have a lot fewer dark days. Trust me.

LARRY LIVE

Law & Order

Do you watch "Law & Order?"

It's on 35 times a week. I don't know how you're NOT watching this show.

"Law & Order" is actually one of those shows I have never seen from beginning to end. I'm always either running late and I miss the beginning, or I start watching it and the phone rings. Or something happens and I miss the ending.

Basically, I've seen "Law." And I've seen "Order." But I've never seen "Law & Order."

So what happens is that I see the crime at the start of the show, but I have no idea what happens to the criminal. I walk around nervous for days. Because, you know, the killer could still be out there!

Or I miss the crime and I only see the trial. The guy gets life in prison and I'm thinking: that seems harsh. But then again, I have no idea what it is he actually did.

I love that every episode of "Law & Order" starts exactly the same way. It's always innocent people doing innocent things and you KNOW within 30 seconds they're going to find a dead body.

You know within 20 feet of where they are, someone's been killed.

It's always something cute, too, like two elderly women playing tennis at an upscale resort. They're hitting the ball back and forth and the ball rolls into the bushes.

"I'll get it, Misty!"

She prances over, opens the bushes and sees a leg!!

The screen goes blank and there's that sound . . .

CHUNG-CHUNG

The next scene is always the police showing up with the lead detective, who used to be played by Jerry Orbach.

I loved the lines they gave Jerry Orbach. Always some awful pun.

There's Jerry Orbach standing on the tennis court, looking down at the dead body. And he says, "Looks like the score wasn't love-all."

CHUNG-CHUNG

What IS that sound? I LOVE that sound! I wish I had that sound as part of my everyday life!

"Bob, I'll be right back. I have to go to that meeting downtown."

CHUNG-CHUNG

CHAPTER 14

PICKING UP THE PIECES

The sad, empty feeling that engulfed me after the Improv closed lasted for months.

"Where do I go now?" was the question that constantly rattled around in my head.

The only other club in town was the Baltimore Comedy Factory above Burke's Café downtown, and I hadn't performed there in the past.

When the Improv was in business, a local comic pretty much had to choose between playing the Improv and playing the Comedy Factory. It was like a Bloods vs. Crips thing. You gave your allegiance to one or the other for bookings and a paycheck, if not other forms of protection.

To be honest, I was afraid of the Comedy Factory.

I had heard it was a rougher audience, a much tougher room to play. It was known for giving out all-you-can-drink coupons, for one thing. Which meant that around 11 o'clock on a weekend night, the place was not exactly packed with clear-eyed Fulbright scholars eager to hear a nuanced, sophisticated brand of humor.

But I reached out to the club and the owners were kind enough to book me as an emcee, which meant I was pretty much starting all over again.

In fact, after I did a killer set at the Ram's Head in Annapolis, one of the Factory bookers who had been in the audience came up to me and said: "Dude, I'm so sorry I'm booking you as an emcee. I'm embarrassed that you're not featuring for us. Let's change that."

I did well performing at the Factory from the very beginning. Within a few months, it became my home club.

Yes, the crowds were a little more, um, chatty than the ones at the Improv. And there was no green room to hang out in between sets.

But the audiences were always good to me. They were different from the Improv: a strange and potent mix of young people simply out for a good time, drunken yahoos and genuine comedy fans.

One of my best shows at the Factory was actually with an audience that couldn't hear me. The club had booked a party of 100 deaf people and they had an interpreter actually *on* the stage with me during my act to sign my jokes.

At one point, I was getting bigger laughs from that group than I was the rest of the crowd. Incredulous, I turned to the interpreter and yelled "Are you even doing my act over there?!" It killed.

When the club decided to put on its own Funniest Person in Baltimore contest, they asked me to run it and I did, willingly. It represented a nice full circle with my past. Now *I* was the one getting to see all these young comics get their start the way I had.

A local kid named Ben Rosen, tall, dark-haired and funny, took the stage the first night, and I knew he would win the whole thing. (He eventually did.) He was a natural in front of the microphone. He was likeable and worked clean, and in this regard reminded me of a young me.

Over drinks in Fells Point, I advised him: "Don't do what I did. If you want this career, go for it. But it's not gonna happen here. You could own this town and it won't mean a damn thing."

Ben was serious about his craft, and I guess he listened to me. Eventually he moved to New York, the Mecca of standup, and began working for BuzzFeed and getting every gig he could to sharpen his act.

In short order, I became the Golden Boy at the Comedy Factory.

In 2006, when out-of-town club operators opened a new comedy club called Rascals in the old Improv space at Power Plant Live!, I helped them with some PR stuff and agreed to perform there, too.

The new club held a soft opening and only about 10 people showed up. I had the misfortune of emceeing that opening weekend.

It was like something out of an old Bill Murray lounge-lizard routine on "Saturday Night Live."

"Welcome to Rascals and our soft opening," I said upon taking the stage that first night. "People have asked me: 'What's a soft opening?'"

I paused and swept my hand dramatically around the vast expanse of empty tables.

"*This*," I continued, "is a soft opening."

To the surprise of absolutely no one, Rascals stayed in business less than a year. Now the Factory owners decided to move *their* club into the old Improv space, too. This time I helped them with their marketing plan while also doing gigs for them.

But the new space felt cavernous now.

The old Factory, because it was so much smaller and the stage so much more compressed, helped the comics feel this connection and energy with the crowd.

Even the green room felt different now, like a ghostly relic from a comedy era gone by. The whole thing felt as if they had remade a favorite TV show from back in the day, but with different actors, and now everything was more than slightly off.

I wasn't drawing the crowds I'd been drawing, and finally I stopped getting booked altogether.

Looking back on it now, the only good thing about the Improv closing – and Rascals going under and me leaving the Factory – was that it forced me to work other places and leave my comfort zone.

I explored other outlets and became a weekly on-air contributor for WBAL-AM's morning show with Dave Durian and Media Max, my friend Max Weiss from *Baltimore Magazine,* who recommended me for the gig. Doing jokes on the radio was a much different experience than working clubs because I didn't have that immediate audience reaction to gauge if the material was working or not. So after each show, I'd call my friend and Harbor Magic colleague, Dennis Morris, on the phone to do a post-show analysis.

I became more bold and adventurous and went on to play clubs in Washington D.C., Philadelphia, New Jersey and Ohio.

And I rededicated myself to going for it more – well, sort of – in the Big Apple.

If conquering New York was still the Holy Grail for most comics, I'd give it a shot – at least in my own way.

LARRY LIVE

More Random Thoughts

Just bought a shirt at the Under Armour outlet. It was the loose style. And I took back a large and an extra large to try on. I don't think I'm truly in touch with the brand #iwillprotectmygut #meatballsub.

***

You know how certain items of clothing just don't fit you any more? And you realize no matter what you do . . . how much you watch what you eat . . . your body has changed and you're never going to get to wear that item again? Well, that finally happened to me . . . I'll miss you underoos . . .

***

I just bought a pumpkin pie at Wegmans and told the kid at the checkout how I had been craving pumpkin pie since last night and was happy to see they had them. Then I realized I was really over-explaining my pie purchase. He looked liked a fan boy, so I made up a joke about how it was my pumpkin pie origins story. And that while I had one at Thanksgiving, I was recasting and re-launching the pumpkin pie franchise with a new vision. It played very well. Big laughs. That's what you call niche comedy. Side note. I forgot to buy the fucking Cool Whip.

***

In a press conference today, Bill Belichick threw Tom Brady under the bus. Brady wasn't hurt, however, as the tires on the bus were . . . well . . . you know.

***

I hope we have a cold winter . . . so all this summer weight I gained wasn't for nothing.

***

So we're driving this morning and the song "Turn Down for What" came on, which I like but didn't know what it meant. So my girlfriend Googled it.

On her iPhone.

In a Mini Cooper.

While driving to Hershey Park.

Whitest . . . Moment . . . Ever.

***

I believe Ray Lewis' pre-game WHAT TIME IS IT?!?! cry was originally just an angry response to Daylight Savings Time.

***

On the flight this morning, the woman next to me had a prayer book and she was reading some safety passages as everyone boarded. After sitting for a while, the pilot made the announcement that they feared a gas leak in the engine and we had to return to the gate.

I turned to the woman and said, "Try harder."

***

I was going to start the 30-Day Ab challenge tonight. But, of course, of all nights, the McDonald's drive thru took FOREVER. Never enough hours in the day.

***

I was excited to give a friend a little present congratulating him on their new baby. I bought this cute blue Polo onesie. A blue bag. A blue card. I even wrote in the card "Congrats on your new baby boy!" The thing is . . . they had a girl. Does Hallmark have a "Sorry I thought your new baby girl was a dude!" section?

***

Driving home I saw something in the middle of the road. It looked like a cat so I slowed down because I didn't want to kill it. I came to a full stop with my lights shining on it. It was then that the "thing" turned its head revealing it was an OWL. And he stared right at me. To avoid anything getting hurt, I blared my horn. At which point, the owl started to sort of walk away . . . dragging a dead bunny to the side of the road.

So I wasn't a killer . . . but I was an accomplice.

***

My doctors called me this morning and told me some of my numbers were high and I should watch what I eat . . . so I had a corned beef sandwich with a cream soda for lunch. Fuck the man.

***

Scenes from Target: Deciding between two lines, I choose poorly. The guy in front of me decides to divide his purchase as each item was rung up, directing the cashier: "This bag . . . that bag . . . this bag." Item by item. I was buying Cheerios and a box of pasta. I asked for two separate bags and the cashier didn't get it. Which was salt in the wound.

CHAPTER 15

"OH, YOU THINK YOU'RE A COMEDIAN?"

I have always had a love-hate relationship with New York, dating back to my first nerve-wracking open-mic night at the New York Comedy Club and as a 17-year-old summer intern with HBO a few years later.

Walking the bustling streets of Manhattan under the towering backdrop of scores of skyscrapers, feeling the energy and excitement of one of the greatest cities in the world, I have never felt more exhilarated – and also more insignificant, a blip in a teeming mass of get-outta-my-way, I'm-headed-straight-to-the-top humanity.

I always felt like the town owned me, and not the other way around.

But by 2006, with the Baltimore Improv closed, I started looking for more opportunities in the Big Apple.

Every comic has the dream of making it there, and making it in Baltimore didn't seem to be in the cards for me. No one's going to hand you success. You have to go get it. And it was becoming clearer and clearer to me that if I wanted to make a name for myself in this business, I had to go where the bright lights were – even if it was the toughest place in the world to play.

At the legendary comedy venue Caroline's on Broadway, I met a man named Andy Engle and was introduced to the singular concept known as the "bringer show."

A "bringer show" means that as long as you bring 10 people to the show who will pay the cover charge and the two-drink minimum, you get your five or six minutes on stage. It helps a club fill what would otherwise be a dead night.

Most comics have conflicted feelings about these "bringer shows."

Sure, they're a step up from open-mic nights. And in my case, it was a chance to play one of the top comedy clubs and maybe have someone in the industry see my act, like it and open another door for me.

On the other hand, with a room packed mostly with the guests of the other comedians, what are the realistic odds of a major club booker, talent scout or TV producer being in the audience?

Instead of, say, Bernie the plumber from Queens and his buddies? All of whom are now officially – let's just come out and say it – shit-faced.

Nonetheless, I sent Engle a tape of some of my gigs and a press kit with all my clippings, and I got booked.

And I didn't just bring 10 people to that first gig. I brought 40.

I had a lot of friends in New York at the time that showed up to see me. And my friends and colleagues from the Baltimore hotel industry drove up to see me, too, as did a number of travel writers I knew.

Engle must have looked at the crowd and thought he died and went to heaven.

It helped that I did really well that first night, too. No, I did better than that. I *killed*. And when you kill at a place like Caroline's, you go from an audience reaction of "Oh, you think you're a comedian?" to "Oh, you're a *comedian!*"

I guess I impressed Andy Engle, too, because the vibe he gave off after the show was that I had proved myself.

I remember leaving Caroline's after that first night and standing in Times Square with all my friends, gazing at the crowds and the twinkling neon lights of Broadway and the cabs whizzing by and thinking: *Wow, I just performed at Caroline's! Fuck if it's a "bringer." It's Caroline's!"*

Then we all went to a bar to celebrate. I've always been blessed with having many loyal friends. That's why, even to this day, I don't know if the full-time comedian's life is for me. Because I've lived a fairly normal life and done comedy. But I haven't been a comedian who's had just a semblance of a life.

Comedians can be loners and neurotics. They travel a lot. There's no home, and that can be a cancer. I like going out, but I like having a home base, too.

I like having the staff at my Starbucks making my coffee drink before I even park the car. I like the fact that the toll lady on I-95 recognizes me and sings out: "Hi, Sugar, how you doing?"

Over the next two years, Engle booked me for quite a few "bringer" showcases at Caroline's – at least a half-dozen. His line to me was: "If I had 100 Larry Notos, my life would be perfect." And I'm sure he meant it, too.

To me, though, the logistics of performing in New York were daunting.

A typical itinerary read like this: get up at 6 in the morning in Bel Air. Commute to my job in Baltimore at the Admiral Fell Inn. Work a full day. Leave around 4 in the afternoon and catch the train to Manhattan.

Walk blocks and blocks and blocks to get to Caroline's. Perform. Stay overnight at a hotel and get maybe three hours sleep. Get on the train at 4 or 5 the next morning to be back at my desk in Baltimore for another full day of work.

One time I remember everything – absolutely *everything* – going wrong.

I dropped my coffee all over my lap. I got to New York in the middle of a driving rainstorm and didn't have an umbrella.

I tried hailing a cab and none of them stopped. So now I'm sloshing through the rain and a taxi blows past, hits a puddle and I get even more drenched.

All this for six minutes on stage!

All this for trying to tell jokes for a lousy six minutes!

You talk about having a balance in life. I don't know what I had back then, but it sure wasn't balance.

One time I was going on vacation with my parents and my sister and her husband. I woke up in Bel Air and drove to Penn Station in Baltimore, where I left my car. From there I took a cab to BWI and a plane to Providence, R.I., where I had meetings all day.

Late that afternoon, I took a train from Providence to Manhattan, where I auditioned for the Montreal Just for Laughs Festival. (The bookers had seen me at Caroline's.)

I did OK in the audition, went out to dinner with some people that night, and took a 3 a.m. train back to Baltimore's Penn Station, where my car was parked. I got in the car and drove to Bel Air, where my mom and sister were waiting with their luggage.

I took my luggage out of my car, threw it in my mom's car and drove that car to BWI, where we all got on a plane and flew to Disney World in Orlando.

But playing New York was a valuable experience for me. For a time, I seemed to be getting a bit of traction there.

After seeing me at Caroline's, CBS Prime Time Casting called. They bring people in to read scripts so they can have you on camera and on file in their library. That way when they need to fill a character's role on a program, they can scroll through their database and see who fits best.

They sent me a script from a sitcom that hadn't been picked up years earlier. I hated it. The character in the script was a real snarky, sarcastic guy. Totally not me.

But that Friday, I dutifully took the train up to New York, with all my family and friends thinking: *This is it! He's going to be the next Ray Romano!*

It didn't quite work out that way.

The setting alone was intimidating: the famed "Black Rock" CBS building on West 52nd Street near Sixth Avenue, where the offices featured names on the doors of venerable programs like "60 Minutes" and "Late Night with David Letterman."

This wasn't Power Plant Live! No, this was where the heavy-hitters worked, the people who could change your life.

I was nervous as hell, to tell the truth.

But I read the script and everything went . . . fine.

You want them to say, in that millisecond after you finish, that you've got it. You want them to say that you're sharp and funny and talented and way better than the millions of other people who've auditioned.

But instead, they say, "Thanks for coming." Then they stick your tape up on a shelf, where it will no doubt gather dust and cobwebs with the tapes of the scores of other self-deluded "super-talents" who read the exact same script.

No, I never got another call back from CBS.

Apparently, the "Everybody Loves Larry" show would have to wait.

But soon after, I did get a guest spot on a Thursday and Sunday at Caroline's for a Louis CK show, which also didn't work out real well.

The crowd was very young and kind of rough. The emcee did a lot of drug and college humor. And here I was in my dress pants and button-down shirt, about to riff about my grandmother and growing up Italian.

I did my weddings and funerals routine and it got just an OK laugh. So I followed with another line: "OK, now I feel like I'm at my own funeral . . ."

When it was over, I was really, really down on myself. A waitress came up to me and said: "I don't know why you said that about your funeral. I thought you did great!"

It cheered me up, but only a little.

Within weeks, my New York experience wound down to a close.

The whole thing was getting way too expensive, costing me literally hundreds of dollars each time I performed there. Sure, if I had made it in New York, I'd be a lot more famous than I am now. But I also think it would have been a life filled with a ton of rejection and frustration.

And that was a trade-off that was never going to work for me.

LARRY LIVE

The Gym

I've gained a little weight.

I know I gained weight because my Italian mother went from saying: "Eat something . . . eat for God's sake!" to "Hmmm, maybe you shouldn't have thirds . . ."

When I go into a clothing store, I have to ask if they have this shirt in a Tony Soprano.

Apparently I'm the size between "Fuhgedaboutit" and "Bada Bing."

So I joined a gym.

I hate the gym. Hate everything about it.

I belong to a gym that only costs $10 a month and is open 24 hours a day. That's the highest amount I'm willing to invest in my ability to actually show up there. And I like to go in the middle of the night so no one sees me.

I don't even know why I'm there.

I see two types of people in the gym: really obese people and people in tremendous shape. And I like to think as much as I don't go, I'm never going to look THAT bad. And I sure as hell know I'll never go enough to look that GOOD.

So why the hell am I here?

I should go home and eat a meatball sub. 'Cause a meatball sub has never hurt me. Or tried to change me as a person.

The exercise machines at the gym don't even have settings for things I'm interested in.

I'm on the elliptical and the settings are like: Do you want to run a marathon? NO!

Do you want to climb a mountain? NO!

All I want to do is have sex without wheezing.

Where's the setting for that?

CHAPTER 16

ROLLING THE DICE – AND FINALLY A PAYOFF

Around this time in my life, I began to put my comedy career in perspective.

A defining moment occurred on the drive down to a club called Ram's Head On Stage in Annapolis, where I was to open for Brad Garrett.

At some point in the 90-minute trip, it occurred to me that Brad Garrett had his own comedy club in Las Vegas.

As usual, I started ruminating about this.

I remember saying to myself: of *course* you want him to book you in Vegas.

Of *course* you want to go back to that Richard Lewis fantasy, where the big-time comic, instead of waving bye-bye after yet another Baltimore gig and beating a hasty retreat out of town to some more glamorous comedy Mecca, turns to you and says: "Come with me, kid. You're funny, kid. I'm gonna make you a star."

But this time, I quickly pulled back from that non-productive reverie.

This time I told myself: don't worry about anything but tonight.

Enjoy the moment. Soak it all in.

And whatever happens, happens.

The truth was, I had taken a number of risks with my comedy up to this point, had gone for stardom in a number of different ways besides just playing local clubs and hoping to be discovered. And for a variety of reasons, none of those risks had panned out.

For starters, I had tried out for the "Last Comic Standing," NBC's so-called "comedy competition."

When people find out you're a comedian, they invariably respond in one of two ways. Either they say, "Tell me a joke," or they say, "Ever think about trying out for 'Last Comic Standing?'" (Yeah, like that had never occurred to me.)

In any event, I *did* try out for the show, just before its second season in 2006. The auditions were held in Boston. I flew up in the middle of winter and stayed in a hotel near historic Faneuil Hall.

On a bitter-cold January morning, I woke up at 4 a.m. and joined hundreds of comedians in line outside a near-by comedy club. All of them were doing what I was doing: taking a risk and following a dream.

The preliminary competition had an assembly-line quality to it. People would finally get to the front of the line and enter the building, only to emerge a few minutes later looking either sad and disgusted or euphoric at having moved on to the second round of cuts.

It felt like a firing squad version of Russian roulette.

Even if you survived at first, they were going to spin the chamber and shoot again. And this time someone else would go down. All you're trying to do is die later than the comic next to you.

The, ahem, "competition" was also rife with favoritism. We saw one comedian rushed to the front of the line because he had a manager who had a relationship with the club. I was told this was not exactly an aberration, either.

Gee, connections and influence skewing what was supposed to be a fair and impartial contest – when had that ever happened before?

In any event, I took a metaphorical bullet moments after taking the stage, when I began with my "Italian weddings and funerals" routine and was quickly cut off.

"You're telling stories," one of the judges said disdainfully.

No, shit, I thought. Hadn't I been told by a number of top comedians that they loved the bit? That it was an old-school classic and they could see why audiences identified with it?

But apparently it didn't fit the vapid, six-second-punch-line, short-attention-span mode that network TV covets. So the judges, whose job is to be snarky assholes anyway, quickly sent me on my way.

It was a crushing blow to my ego. Back outside in the freezing weather, I was reeling.

I called Tara Lynn at the Improv from the Boston airport, feeling I was now officially a failure and loser who was wasting his time in the business. Thank God she gave me a good pep talk, thereby ensuring that I didn't spend the entire flight home curled up in the fetal position and sobbing.

A few years later, I took another big gamble and went for it again. My new comedy home in Baltimore was Magooby's Joke House in Timonium and I was doing well there. But like my Improv days, one club in one town does not a career make.

There was an agent at the Funny Bone in Columbus, Ohio who booked comedians at around 20 different major clubs throughout the country. You had to get an addition, do well, get "passed" (meaning he would book you) and then pray you actually got booked.

After a *year* of emailing, I finally got a date for an audition. I flew to Ohio, got a rental car, worked all day in my hotel room for my day job and then drove to the club to try and be put on the "to be booked list." No build up and no pressure at all.

The women who went up before me bombed. Crickets. Meaning I went up in front of a dead crowd. But I killed. The agent was impressed how fast I was able to get energy into the room so the whole thing worked in my favor.

I got passed and now it was time to be booked. But in two years, the Funny Bone bookers only called me once. And that was for a last-minute gig in Virginia Beach, which I couldn't do because of a schedule conflict.

The truth was, though, that I didn't want to be 20 years in this business and going from Magooby's to the Funny Bone in Columbus to the Sidewinders in Indiana to the Chuckle Hut in whatever hick town *that's* in – that wasn't happiness for me.

At this point, I was also feeling stuck in my role as the ever-cheerful and pliant opening act.

I've always felt that in life, there were lead actors and there were extras, and I never wanted to be an extra.

I've always wanted to leave my mark on the world. But I sure hadn't achieved that yet.

But in 2010, a shot at the big-time seemed to present itself again.

It began innocuously enough with an email from Ram's Head On Stage in Annapolis that said simply: "How would you like to open for Brad Garrett?"

My response, of course, was typically low-key.

"ARE YOU KIDDING?!" I wanted to scream. "I'D COMMIT HOMICIDE TO WORK WITH THAT GUY!"

For one thing, I was a huge fan of "Everyone Loves Raymond," one of my favorite sitcoms of all time. I had met Doris Roberts, who played Raymond's mom on the show, at an Italian-American gala in Washington, D.C., and found her to be a lovely woman. And I had always loved Ray Romano's standup act, identifying with all the jokes about growing up in an Italian family.

As for Brad Garrett, I had always thought he played one of the greatest sitcom characters of all time as Ray Romano's sad-sack brother. So I was super-amped to meet him, even though on the drive to the club, the yellow caution light in my brain kept flashing: *Easy, big guy. Whatever happens, happens.*

It was just me and Brad on the bill that night. But since there were two green rooms, I didn't get to see him before I went on.

I thought I did well enough with my 15 minutes on stage. It wasn't a killer set, but it was respectable.

After that I introduced Brad Garrett. It was my first time actually meeting him – and the man couldn't have been nicer.

He motioned for me to remain on stage with him and soak in the applause. He seemed very genuine, looking me right in the eye the whole time.

He even used me as a comic foil in his act. I had forgotten to raise the mic stand when he went on, and because he's so tall, the mic came up to about his nipples. So he did the first five minutes of his act with the mic at that level, talking softly and even pantomiming jokes.

In between shows, he came into my dressing room. He was in a playful mood, cracking jokes the whole time, and it was like we had known each other forever.

"You did a nice job," he told me. "You're really funny."

I thought he was just being nice and waved him off with a murmured "thanks."

"No, really," he went on. "I was watching you from the back of the room. And I turned to my friend and said: 'I'm fucked. This kid's gonna make me work tonight.' My friend said you did a really great job, too."

He paused for a moment.

"Ever play Vegas?" he continued. "You should come out and do a week in Vegas. I'd love to have you at my club . . ."

A few of my friends were standing nearby and happened to overhear this. When Brad left, they were practically jumping up and down with excitement.

"Did he just say that?!" they shouted. "Oh, my God, we're all going to Vegas!"

After we did the second show, Brad ran into my dressing room and said: "I gotta get out of here – early flight tomorrow. Do you have something with your info on it?"

I handed him a flyer with my email address.

"I'll have Elaine call you," Brad said, running out the door. "Great job, kid."

And with that, he was gone.

Wait a minute, I thought. Is he serious about me coming to Vegas? Sure sounded that way . . .

The next day, at my office in the Admiral Fell Inn, I kept refreshing my email every five minutes, waiting for a message from Elaine, whoever she was.

Sure enough, it finally arrived.

Elaine introduced herself as working for a talent agency in the Midwest.

"Brad contacted me before he got on the plane," she wrote. "He'd like you to appear at his club in Las Vegas for a week. What are your avails in the next year?"

What are my *avails?!* To play Brad Garrett's club in Vegas?!

How about I'm available all of fucking 2011! No, check that. I am available to play the Brad Garrett cabaret – on any night of his choosing – for the rest of my fucking life!

OK, I didn't respond in exactly that manner to Elaine.

Instead, I replied with a cleaner, more restrained version, thanking her and Brad for thinking of me and listing a whole bunch of available dates.

But she never emailed back.

A week went by. Two weeks. I sent another email. No response.

Finally after a month, she emailed to say she had my info. But Brad's club was a really tough club to get into, she wrote. Nevertheless, she'd keep me posted on her efforts.

I figured I wouldn't hear from her for another six months. Or maybe a year.

Or maybe ever.

But three months later, at 1 in the morning, just as I was about to go to bed, I heard a ding on my iPad.

And there it was: I could play Brad's club the September week of Labor Day. It's located, she wrote, in the Tropicana Las Vegas hotel, right on the world-famous Strip.

In a heartbeat, I jumped at the opportunity.

Labor Day was a bad time to leave my day job working for Harbor Magic. Baltimore was hosting its first big Grand Prix race through the streets around the Inner Harbor. And I was on the marketing committee, tasked with finding ways to draw race spectators to town.

But when I asked my boss, Ken, for permission to go out of town for a comedy gig at such a critical time, he said: "You gotta do this, right?"

I nodded. Yep, I gotta do this.

"Then go do it," he said. What a great guy. Ken knew what it meant to me.

So I flew out to Vegas with my mom, a day early since there was now a hurricane bearing down on Baltimore. A host of my relatives, friends and former colleagues had indicated they were flying out to see me, too.

But I wouldn't let anyone attend the show the first night. I wanted to get used to the room without the added pressure of seeing familiar faces in the audience.

It's not that I was really nervous, either. I was at the point in my career where I had found my confidence, where I approached every gig with the mindset of: *Ok, let's get on stage and do it! Let's punch 'em in the mouth and do it!*

On the other hand, I was also curious as to how the audience would react to my act.

The room itself was an old ballroom about the size of the Comedy Factory that held maybe 300 people on the weekend. But this was a club that landed A-list talent and billed itself as "home to the best comedy on the Las Vegas Strip!"

Up to this point, I had primarily worked East Coast clubs. There's an East Coast brand of humor that I always thought to be edgier, hipper, even darker than the humor found everywhere else.

Would a Vegas audience comprised ostensibly of vacationers and gamblers from all over the country – and the world – laugh at "Italian weddings and funerals?"

I was about to find out.

Bottom line: I did great.

I shared the bill with an emcee and comedian/actor Ralph Harris. We did eight shows Monday through Saturday. I did 25 minutes of standup for each show. And in one of the hottest (literally and figuratively) comedy towns on the map, I killed.

And the best part was this: I got to share the whole experience with all my family and friends.

Look, if I had been a regular comedian, I would have spent the whole week in Vegas by myself, eating my meals alone in the hotel kitchen every night the way people in this business do.

Instead, I was taking in the sights with friends, eating meals in four-star restaurants with family members – and finding love and support in the audience every night when I took the stage and gazed into their faces.

There was my family from Maryland and Pennsylvania. There was Lee Rose, a PR colleague from Fort Myers, Florida, who flew out to surprise me. Lee and I had met at a conference in Canada over ten years ago. He seemed shy at first, but eventually revealed he used to be on a morning radio show. He did his impression of Bob Hope and Johnny Carson. I sang Sinatra and did Jerry Lewis. And we've been friends ever since.

There were James and Julie Dempsey from California, who I had met in line at a Disney convention in Anaheim. Genevieve Adell, an aspiring actress who had helped me rehearse for that CBS audition, who drove from LA. There was my honorary Italian fan club from Baltimore lead by Michelle Petti and Chicky Peluso. Former colleagues from Harbor Magic and Visit Baltimore. And Tom Wynkoop from Channel 2. Tom and I had dinner at Sinatra restaurant at the

Wynn hotel, then drove the strip talking about the Rat Pack, movies and girls.

All these wonderful people had spent their own hard-earned money on airline tickets, hotel reservations and rental cars just to be at the Tropicana for me.

"We'll have you back in a year!" the manager told me when the week was up.

The booker, though, never gave me a date, saying there was high demand from comics trying to play the place for the first time. So I never went back.

Yet what I took away from the week was not the old anxiety about taking the next step toward being a big star. I wasn't frustrated or unhappy.

What I was left with instead was a genuine appreciation for my good fortune and the great memories I'd always have of working the Vegas Strip – by far the highlight of my comedy career.

What humbled me, too, was that I had so many amazing people in my life with whom to share the experience.

I don' know if there are too many other comedians who can say that.

But at least I can.

LARRY LIVE

Burger King

I hate Burger King.

HATE.

First of all, I don't know who thought bringing the king to life in these commercials was a good a idea! This plastic weirdo freak running around a football field does NOT make me crave a Whopper.

And they had KIDS' Halloween costumes!!!

"What do you want to be for Halloween this year? Spider Man? A Ninja Turtle?"

"I want to be the Burger King!"

Burger King's slogan is just a blatant lie – HAVE IT YOUR WAY.

I've never . . . ever . . . had it my way.

I've REQUESTED it my way. Never happened.

It's the worst drive-thru known to mankind.

I honestly think they throw random ingredients in the air and whatever happens to land on the bun is what you get.

Their wrappers actually have "PLACE SANDWICH HERE" printed on them to help guide workers.

It's a wrapper!!! Where the hell else are you going to put the sandwich?!!?

I went to the Burger King drive- thru once and asked for a Whopper PLAIN.

I guess I really stressed the plain part and the employee was feeling like a smart ass. Because when I drove away, I opened up the wrapper and it was JUST THE BREAD.

Can you imagine the level of fury that wells up inside you when you have to turn the car around, drive back to the Burger King, park, walk in, stand in line and ask for MEAT!!?!!

I went to the Burger King drive-thru once and drove up to the speaker expecting the absolute worst.

But I was pleasantly surprised as a very eloquent, classy voice came over the speaker.

"Welcome to Burger King. May I take your order please?"

My jaw dropped and I smiled and thought to myself: Wow, Burger King. You're really stepping up your game.

What I didn't know was that it was a recording . . . and apparently they didn't record any follow up questions . . .

"Oh yes. I'll take a number three with a Coke . . ."

"YOU WANT FRIES WITH THAT, MOTHER FUCKA!!!"

Whatever happened to Jeeves???

CHAPTER 17

BEHIND THE SCENES: IT CAN GET UGLY

The structure of a comedy show is generally the same from gig to gig. Almost every one has a beginning, a middle, and an end: the emcee, feature and headliner.

And the emcee – who knows this better than me? – has a tough job.

As soon as he takes the stage, he has to deal with the unspoken vibe in the room: *who's this guy?*

Before you tell your first joke, the audience is staring at you with a mixture of curiosity, mild suspicion and – if they're already loaded and predisposed to this sort of thing – latent hostility.

You can see it in their faces: is this guy funny? How funny can he be if he's only the opening act?

Where's the guy we *really* came to see?

So your job is to warm them up and make them relax and have a good time – no small task.

For one thing, people are often still being seated as you begin your act. Maybe they've been cooling their heels in a tight hallway or staircase waiting for a table, which doesn't exactly put them in a terrific mood.

Now the waitress is taking their drink orders, which means the emcee's act proceeds amid a steady backdrop of murmurs: "Yo, I'll take a Bud Light," and "What kind of white wine do you have?"

Oh, yeah, that'll really help your concentration – especially if you're new at this sort of thing and nervous as hell to begin with.

Not that everything is a piece of cake for the headliner, either.

The check drop hurts the headliner – no question about that. Brian Regan used to say: why can't they wait until the show's over to bring the check to each table?

On a tight turnaround after the first show on a two-show night, that's probably not practical. Plus the headliner already has the pressure of being the act people came to see. And after people have already sat through 40 minutes of comedy, the headliner has the daunting task of keeping them engaged for another hour or so.

To me, the feature, the No. 2 performer, was always the sweet spot in the lineup. The audience has settled in, they're basking in the glow caused by a competent emcee and alcohol, and they're ready to have a good time.

Plus you don't have to be great – they're here to see the other guy.

I always hate when people say: "Oh, you were funnier than the headliner." But that's often because people had expectations – that might not have been met – of the headliner's act. Whereas my act, if it was any good, might have come as a pleasant surprise.

People always ask me if I get hecklers. And the answer is: usually not. C'mon, with my choirboy looks and friendly demeanor? It would be like heckling a golden retriever.

What I *do* get, though, are people talking a lot in the middle of my act. One time I actually snapped and yelled "SHUT THE FUCK UP!" to people talking when I worked the Comedy Factory.

They weren't talking *at* me, they were talking to each other. Loudly. The bouncers are supposed to take care of that problem, but they weren't doing their job. And the people wouldn't shut up. Which is the main reason I went psycho on their rude asses.

The rest of the audience applauded this, by the way. And a few minutes later, when those customers starting talking again, the bouncers tossed them out.

The fact is, serial talkers are an endless source of frustration for comics.

What amazes me are people who talk as if they don't understand that there's a show going on. You want to shake them and bark: "Hey, didn't you get the memo? This is a fucking comedy show, you moron!"

Once in the middle of my act at the Comedy Factory, four women were seated in the front row. As soon as they got their food, they began sharing it and commenting on it ("Oh, that's *so* good! What kind of sauce is that?") in voices that got louder and louder.

I started talking about them to the rest of the audience, but they were so focused on the food that they didn't even notice.

Finally one of the women looked up and said: "I'm sorry, but these fried mozzarella sticks are so good!"

"Oh, why didn't you say so!" I said. "You believe this? I just lost out to the fry guy! I worked on this act for 10 years, writing, putting words together in a humorous way, polishing my act."

"But a guy drops cheese into a vat of hot oil, and *he* won out!"

The audience loved it. Even the mozzarella-stick fan club cracked up. It became my favorite ad-lib of all time, even though I'm not big on interrupting the flow of my act for that sort of thing.

Then there are the audience members who sit there stone-faced with their arms crossed, as if they're determined not to have a good time.

It's almost as if they're angry or upset in some way that they're there. Here again, you want to say: "What the fuck is wrong with you? Do you really hate life so much that you're just gonna sit there with that sourpuss look on your face?"

People coming in late to the show can also throw things off.

I was doing a show once at Magooby's when an older man in an all-white suit and white hat walked in accompanied by a very attractive African-American woman.

I watched him, and I knew everyone else in the crowd was watching him, too. It was weird: I was still doing my act, my mouth was moving, but my mind was focused on this couple.

And my mind was trying to figure out: who is he? And do I want to go there with some wise-ass comment?

I guess I did.

Because in the next instant, I said: "Truman Capote everybody!"

And it killed! The place exploded in laughter!

For a moment, I thought I'd died and gone to heaven. It was a perfect comedy moment: a quick zinger that worked and then right back into my act without missing a beat.

As for the guy in the white suit and hat, he just smiled and waved. He seemed to enjoy the attention. A man dressed like that – he definitely didn't mind all eyes being on him.

Another thing I get asked all the time: are there such things as comedy groupies?

Uh, not exactly.

See, comedians aren't exactly like rock or hip-hop musicians when it comes to getting women – even though women always profess to want a man with a sense of humor.

And comics are professional funny people, right? If you're a woman and a sense of humor is an important component to what you're looking for in a man, hell, you should be lining up at comedy clubs every night!

But apparently it doesn't work that way.

Once when I was playing at the Baltimore Improv, a woman came up to me after I left the stage and gushed: "Oh, my God, you were *so* funny!"

Then she proceeded to touch my shoulder, which for me is like going all the way! To me, if you touch my shoulder like that, it practically means we're engaged.

"What are you doing after the show?" she asked with a big smile.

"I don't know," I replied. "What are *you* doing?"

"I don't know," she said. "But find me afterwards."

"Oh, I will," I said happily. "I'll hunt you down and find you no matter where you are. Trust me."

So now, of course, I'm thinking: *This is it! I'm in! Here I thought the comedy groupie was only a mythical creature, something from legend and lore. But here's one in the flesh! And she really digs me!*

So after the show, I find her in the lobby. There's the usual post-show buzz, people taking pictures, people saying good-bye to each other, people heading to their cars, etc.

Again, we go through what I can only assume is more pre-coital banter.

"What do you want to do?" she says again.

Naturally, I was ready with a snappy answer.

"I'm cool with wherever you want to go," I said.

And with that – I can see it in my mind's eye like it was yesterday – she turns to the guy next to her and says: "Honey, where do you want to go?"

And the guy turns out to be her goddamn boyfriend!

I'm thinking: *What am I, a monkey? I'm gonna come with you and your boyfriend and just tell jokes? What the fuck!*

Needless to say, I didn't go anywhere with them. But the whole thing was so weird. What did she want me to do, go home with them and watch them have sex and fire off one-liners and funny observations?

To paraphrase the great artist and philosopher Meat Loaf: I'd do anything for love . . .

But I won't do that.

LARRY LIVE

Target

I own a house now, which means I spend most of my free time in Target.

Oh, how I love Target . . .

I walk through the place like it's a state park . . . just strolling through the aisles with my Starbucks, admiring the beauty of the cornucopia of merchandise.

I love the combinations of items you get at Target . . . because you have no plan.

I was in Target once and bought three items: cream puffs, tongs for the grill, and "Juno" on DVD.

And the asshole at the register looked at me like that was my plan all along. Like I came in there for those three specific items . . .

Like I was going to go home, put in "Juno" and eat cream puffs with tongs all night.

If I'm not at Target, you can find me at BJ's Wholesale buying way too much food for a person my size who lives alone.

I should explain why I go there:

First off, do you know that I'm the TALLEST member of my family?

Do you know what it's like to be 5-foot-7 and called "The Great One?"

Anyway, my parents go through bottled water like you wouldn't believe. I think they may be stocking some sort of underground bunker.

But they're so little they can't carry the water. So they ask me to do it.

"Send the muscle to BJ's to get some water." And I'm the muscle.

So I'm in BJ's pushing a pallet of water. Sixteen cases of water. Pushing it through the store like I fill vending machines on the side.

And I'm pushing it and I see a display of donuts.

I like donuts. So I grab a box.

So now I have this giant stack of waters, with this little box of donuts on top. And I get up to the register again. And AGAIN the asshole looks at me like THIS was my plan.

So I look at him and say: "Hey, donuts make me thirsty . . ."

CHAPTER 18

I GOT THIS IDEA . . .

A confession: I have these . . . *things* inside of me that need to come out from time to time.

Oh, it's not like the classic sci-fi movie "Alien" with Sigourney Weaver, where some weird, squishy life form is going to burst from my chest.

Thankfully, it's much more benign. I explained it once as "creative dry-heaving," this over-powering need to share with the world all these ideas I have in my head.

I have a whiteboard in my office where I list all these things I want to do: write a book – OK, we can scratch that one off the list – write screen-plays, start a non-profit to introduce disadvantaged kids to the arts, etc.

Having all these ideas pinging through your brain non-stop is a blessing for a creative person. But it can also be a curse, because you tend to jump from one thing to another and become easily distracted.

On the other hand, it sure is fun when you throw yourself compulsively into a project and it consumes you . . .

Five years ago, for example, I came up with the idea of a Muppets Christmas card.

I was so tired of getting Christmas cards in the mail from all these happy-looking married friends and family members posing with their kids.

Hey, I thought, what about me? I'm not married. And I don't have kids. So what kind of Christmas card do *I* send out?

When you're single, you can't send cards with pictures of yourself. What was I gonna do – send a photo of me updating my match.com profile?

Then it hit me: what about a card with me and the Muppets?

So my friend Maria came over and she photographed me sitting in a brown leather chair in front of a Christmas tree, with all the Muppet characters posed around me as if they were my children.

And the tag line for the card was: "No wife. No kids. No wonder."

I think it's one the funniest things I've created.

I sent the photos to be developed at Walgreens. And when I went to pick them up, the woman behind the counter said: "I don't mean to pry. But I have to ask you: how did you meet the Muppets?"

I didn't have the nerve to tell her that the loveable furry puppet characters were from my own, ahem, private collection. That I had a room stocked with Muppets and another room devoted to Disney characters.

So I came up with a story about being on tour and doing a photo-shoot with the Muppets.

In any event, I sent 300 of the cards out to friends and family, and the response was unbelievable.

Lots of people told me it was the best Christmas card they had ever received. They put it on their refrigerator or displayed it on their mantle or framed it like it was a piece of art. It brought people so much joy – and brought me so much joy, too.

To see the creative process through – to see it go from something abstract in your mind to something tangible, even though it was a silly little Christmas card – was a great feeling. And if I died tomorrow, that photo of me and the Muppets was the one I'd want them to use at my funeral.

The next creative brainstorm to form in my feverish little head came as a direct result of being a life-long Orioles fan. If Disney World is my favorite place on Earth – and it is – Camden Yards is probably no. 2 on the list.

But in 2010, the Orioles were struggling, mired in a woeful streak of 13 straight losing seasons. The fan base was discouraged and depressed. Attendance at the stadium plummeted. When Dave Trembley was fired as manager halfway through the season and replaced a month later by Buck Showalter, I had mixed feelings.

What difference does a new manager make? I thought. *No one's going to come in here and change things. We're doomed. Cursed to be a crappy team forever.*

Then this cocksure, demanding little man, this second coming of the sainted Earl Weaver, this Showalter, seemed to change the culture of the club overnight. The Orioles rattled off an impressive winning streak right away. And in the last month of the season, they had the second-best record in the American League.

By September, I was firing emails to my mom that played off an idea I kept turning over in my head: that while the New York Yankees' payroll was an astronomical $220 million, Baltimore only needed one "Buck" to turn things around.

A die-hard Orioles fan herself, my mom urged me to do something with the slogan – if that's even what it was at the time.

I didn't do much at first. But as the 2011 season approached and it was clear that the Orioles' entire publicity and marketing campaign centered around their feisty new manager, I finally figured out what to do with the "In Buck We Trust" slogan: slap it on a T-shirt.

I went to my neighbor, Garth Gerhart, a talented graphic designer and cartoonist for *Mad* magazine, who agreed to design the shirts. Garth and I were like polar opposites. He didn't know anything about baseball. An Army vet, he's married with two kids, doesn't give a shit what people think of him and posts all sorts of crazy things – some offensive – on Facebook.

Me, I'm the one with the Disney room in my house. And the Muppets room. If you didn't know that, though, you'd have looked at the two of us and said: Garth's the single guy and Larry's the married guy.

Just didn't work out that way.

In any event, we pitched the T-shirt idea to a company called SwagDog, which deals in licensed apparel manufacturing of shirts, hoodies and hats. I wrote a press release and sent it to the media.

WJZ-TV, the local CBS affiliate, mentioned our T-shirts on their evening news and I did an interview with radio talk-show host Mark Viviano of 105.7 The Fan. The Orioles did the rest, opening on the road, sweeping Tampa Bay and returning to Camden Yards for their home opener with the whole town buzzing.

On Opening Day, FOX-45 TV interviewed Garth and I about the shirts early that morning on the field.

We also did interviews with a couple of other stations, as well as the *Baltimore Business Journal* and the *Sun*. We arrived at the ballpark around 5 a.m. and entered through the private security entrance. As Garth and I made our way through the bowels of Camden Yards, down narrow hallways, we half-joked that Buck was going to jump out of one of the doors and beat us with a baseball bat for using his image without his permission. Luckily, we made our way to the field without any surprise muggings from the manager.

The T-shirts were getting some major publicity. Now all we had to do is actually sell some of them.

That day, I was dragging around a suitcase full of shirts that we planned to sell outside on the streets. Except . . . I promptly realized I was terrible at sales.

I would stand on a corner outside the stadium, holding up the shirts and people wouldn't even look at me. I don't know if it was because I was too timid or too self-conscious or what.

Whatever the reason, I started getting a feeling that this was all a horrible mistake, that the T-shirts were going to bomb and we wouldn't sell any and – at $14.99 each – we'd lose a ton of money on them.

But then my buddy Ben Rosen, that same young comic who I had befriended at the Comedy Factory contest and who wasn't self-conscious in the least, started walking up to people and hawking the shirts. And next thing I knew, Ben and a friend were selling the hell out of our Buck shirts! They also were sold in local sports stores and at the gift shop of the Sports Legends Museum next to Camden Yards.

The shirts would go on to sell like hotcakes. In fact, we sold thousands of the shirts in just a few weeks time. And they were mentioned frequently on ESPN and the MLB Network.

Then sales just . . . stopped.

The problem was that the Orioles reverted back to their losing ways, eventually finishing in last place in the AL East with a 69-93 record. Fans quickly stopped caring about the team, as usual.

Oh, sure, the Orioles would make the playoffs the following season, which generated a resurgence of interest in the Buck T-shirts. But the tsunami of sales slowed down.

I would see fans wearing the shirt at games and throughout town. Sometimes I wouldn't say anything, but sometimes I would be excited to introduce myself and tell them my connection to it.

At FanFest, the Orioles annual winter celebration, a girl wearing the shirt told me a story about how Buck had seen her wearing it at an event and loved it. He had even asked her to come up on stage so he could autograph it.

When you get a taste of success, you always want it again. And when you have an idea and you have faith in it and it hits, you think: hell, no reason we can't replicate that.

But when we rolled out our Ravens Retribution T-shirts in 2012, we found out how hard it was to catch lightening in a bottle twice.

On paper, it looked like a great idea.

The Ravens had missed a shot at the Super Bowl a year earlier because of a horrendous series of events in the AFC Championship game, low-lighted by a dropped catch by wide out Lee Evans and a shanked chip-shot field goal by kicker Billy Cundiff.

Ravens fans, rightly or wrongly, felt they'd been robbed.

With the Super Bowl in New Orleans that season, we came out with purple T-shirts that said "New Season, New Hope, New Orleans" and under that "Baltimore Football, Retribution 2012.com."

I thought it was, well, inspired on so many levels.

A story line about retribution seemed like a total winner. It spoke to Baltimore's perennial status as a gritty underdog, and the chip on the shoulder the size of a sequoia that its sports fans carried.

We released a promotional video explaining the story line, had the T-shirts designed and made. I got a call from *The Aegis* newspaper in Harford County, which wanted to do a story on the shirts.

Here we go, I thought. The shirts are gonna be a big hit. This is how the Buck shirts took off.

Except . . . it never happened. The press coverage ended right there.

The Ravens' season began with the lingering sense of a letdown, a hangover from the year before. And even though the team would go on to post a 10-6 record and play in the AFC Championship game for the second year in a row, the Ravens Retribution tees failed to generate any buzz.

The funny thing was the Ravens did win the Super Bowl in New Orleans that season. The shirt was ahead of its time, so I had to settle for my team getting a second ring in ten years. Not a bad trade off.

I had high hopes for my next project, too, which I called "The Most Interesting Elf in the World." It was a spoof, of course, of the wildly popular "The Most Interesting Man in the World" commercials for Dos Equis beer.

"The Most Interesting Elf" was pegged to the holiday season, and we hoped SwagDog would aggressively market T-shirts with a caricature of a white-haired, debonair and overly tanned looking elf holding a steaming mug of hot chocolate, topped off with a candy-cane.

My dream was to see the tees land in big chain stores like Target. But that never happened.

I spent my own money printing up "Most Interesting Elf" cards that I sent to the Comedy Central network and to comedy clubs. And I produced a promotional video, in which an off-screen announcer – that would be me – recites tongue-in-cheek praise for the elf in the stentorian tones used in the Dos Equis spots:

"On one foggy night, he led Santa's sleigh with his charm alone."

"He once got eight maids a milking, on a Wednesday in June."

"Snowflakes aim for his tongue."

"Norman Rockwell once posed for him."

"His lists don't have to be checked twice."

"He knows what you want, but you can *still* sit on his lap."

I was proud of the lines and hoped the video would go viral on YouTube. But that never happened, either. Partly, I think, this was due to the fact that the video was made up only of my words flashing on the screen, instead of an actual character that could have been developed.

Whatever the reason, sales were disappointing. And if you're scoring along at home – the way I was in my head – this made two creative disappointments in a row now. And I followed it with a third, a song I wrote called "Twelve Days of Baltimore Christmas" that celebrated iconic local images (blue crabs, Natty Boh beers, Berger cookies, etc.) in a spoof of the popular holiday anthem.

The production of the song was delayed, the vision I had for a animated video never came to be. The song wasn't released until a week before Christmas and failed to take off, leaving me a nifty 0-for-3 in my most recent off-stage projects.

Did I learn my lesson?

Did I finally come to the realization that punishing myself this way was the equivalent of death by a thousand paper cuts?

Uh, no, I did not.

Instead, one morning late in the summer of 2014, with the Orioles in the heat of a pennant race and closing in on the divisional crown, I woke up one morning with another brainstorm.

The song "Let it Go" from the hit Disney movie "Frozen" was running through my head. In some ways, this was to be expected: "Let it Go" was the hottest – some would say most *annoying* – song around.

It was everywhere – you couldn't get away from it if you tried.

Only instead of that drippy chorus of "Let it go-o-o-o, let it go-o-o-o!" the lyrics rattling around in my skull were: "Let's go O-o-o-o's! Let's go O-o-o-o's!"

Oh, my God, I thought. It's perfect!

I texted Garth and my mom to see what they thought of the idea. They loved it. "Do something with it!" they both said.

So I did. I wrote most of the parody song in an hour and half at Towson Town Center while the battery on my cell phone was being replaced.

My friend Michelle Petti, who has a great voice, agreed to sing it. We recorded it with the help of Michelle's mom, Chicky Peluso, and her husband, Rudy D'Antoni.

I edited the video myself, hoping it would go viral. I wanted to be part of the Orioles' fan excitement that was sweeping the city. Part of the playoff buzz.

And the song and video definitely caught on. It was a great parody song. It made a splash right out of the gate. (Eventually, it would attract over 30,000 views.)

But right away, I got hosed again.

(Sigh.)

After sweeping the Detroit Tigers in the playoffs, the Orioles were scheduled to play the Kansas City Royals in the League Championship Series.

Which is when a young, attractive female O's fan came out with a parody of the Lorde song, "Royals."

Decked out in a black Orioles T-shirt on her YouTube video, she delivered a sultry, hypnotic-sounding paean to her hometown and the Orioles, full of defiant lyrics like "What does Kansas City got on us?" and "We'll beat the ROY-allls!" and "See you in the World Series, my friend."

The thing got 10,000 views in a day! And she got massive media coverage – the kind of coverage we got when the "In Buck We Trust" T-shirts debuted.

Honestly, I was depressed. Very depressed. If we hit a double with our song, she hit it out of the park with hers.

When I told my friend Amy Burke Friedman – a local PR guru – how heartsick I was over this turn of events, she said: "Why did you do your song? Did you do it for the notoriety? Or did you do it because you're a fan?"

The truth was, I had done it for both reasons. But her words made me realize that, if nothing else, my song had helped me and hundreds of other Orioles fans enjoy the playoffs even more than we normally would have.

Not only that, but it had gotten a lot of media play. And radio play, too.

Perspective – it's a beautiful thing, if you can find it.

A few days later, another wonderful thing happened.

A friend happened to share my "Let's Go O's" video on Facebook. Her sister, a teacher at St. John the Evangelist School in Severna Park and a die-hard O's fan, began playing it for the students at lunchtime.

Pretty soon, I was getting reports that hundreds of kids at the school were watching the video on a big screen and singing: "Let's go, O-o-o-o-s! Let's go O-o-o-o-s! Win it all for Bal-ti-more!"

I was amazed. Absolutely blown away.

I contacted the school and asked if they'd be interested in me coming down to talk to the kids. They said yes. And on the day of my visit, WBAL-TV sent reporter Jennifer Franciotti to do a story on the event.

It was a great experience – and a great lesson for me.

Maybe that *other* song got 55,000 views and mine only got 30,000. But there could be nothing as heart-warming as seeing all these kids at St. John decked out in Orioles headbands and waving O's flags, singing my song and looking at me like I was some kind of conquering hero.

"He's wearing that Buck shirt!" one kid proclaimed when I walked into the classroom.

After the media left, the teacher had me do a Q & A session with the kids. One of the kids asked me if I had also written "Thank God I'm a Country Boy," which the Orioles play during every seventh inning stretch.

I chuckled and said, "No, that was written by John Denver."

As kids do, the next question came right away: "Who's John Denver?"

I thought as fast as I could as way to connect with these kids. "Oh . . . he did an album with the Muppets."

Oh, they were *very* impressed with Mr. Denver now. I just wish I had had my Christmas card on me.

But the thing I'm most grateful for from that whole experience?

It was this: when I walked into the school to do the media interview, who was sitting behind the reception desk but none other than Sister Marie Gregory, that white-haired angel who changed my life and helped me discover a talent inside me I didn't know I had all those years ago.

We both teared up and embraced. We had spoken a few times and traded a few letters over the years, but had not seen each other in quite some time. She introduced me to everyone using one of her old lines: "This boy was a pain in my back pew."

The media attention, the creative successes, the T-shirt sales – none of it mattered as much as being able to see this great woman. I wanted to make sure I took advantage of the opportunity.

"All of this," I told her, "happened so I could be in here in person to thank you for everything you did for me over the years. I am who I am because of having people like you in my life."

She paused and said: "Trust me, when I tell you, I learned more from you then I ever was able to teach you."

I wanted to argue that I was not deserving of such praise, but I knew better. You don't fight with a nun.

After the Orioles' season ended in a desultory four-game sweep by the Royals, the school sent me a package of mail from the kids.

Many of the letters read something like this: "Thank you for coming. The Orioles lost. I'm sorry. But it will be OK."

Oh my God! I thought. These kids think I'm gonna hang myself!

Instead, I would spend weeks basking in the glow of that awesome day with the kids and Sister Marie in Severna Park, which remains one of the true highlights of my life.

LARRY LIVE

"Wheel of Fortune"

I'd like to talk about "Wheel of Fortune." Why? Because we don't really discuss it enough as a society.

First of all, I think Pat Sajak is going to snap at any moment. How long has he been hosting this show – 80 years?

How long can he go on with those little cards and the three contestants with their stupid pathetic little lives?

Wouldn't it be great to see Pat Sajak snap? He's so calm, cool and collected. You wouldn't even see it coming.

One of the contestants would ask if there was a T . . .

"THERE'S ALREADY A 'T' ON THE BOARD, YOU FUCKING IDIOT!!!"

Whoa, Pat! Take it easy, buddy . . .

It's not even the same show anymore. I watched it the other day and I knew we were in trouble when Pat said: "OK, contestants, pick up your buzzers . . ."

WHAT?! THERE AREN'T ANY BUZZERS ON THE FUCKING "WHEEL OF FORTUNE!!!"

But that's exactly what happened. Each of the contestants had a buzzer in his or her hand, anxiously awaiting the new "Toss-up" round.

This is a new round where letters pop up one by one until someone recognizes the puzzle and buzzes in. There's no spinning of the wheel. There's no strategy of buying vowels. Letters just appear . . . one by one . . . until someone buzzes in to solve it.

THAT'S NOT "WHEEL OF FORTUNE!" YOU KNOW WHAT THAT IS? IT'S CALLED: READING!!!

I also think they're running out of puzzles. They're gone through every phrase and song title. Now they have this new category: Before and After. This is where there are two phrases linked by a common word in the middle.

I didn't even know what this was. I'm watching and people are solving puzzles like:

SCRATCH MY BACK TO SCHOOL

Or

POTATO SKIN CARE PRODUCTS

I thought I'd had a stroke and no one told me.

The thing I really hate about "Wheel of Fortune" is toward the end of the show. Not the bonus round, but when they're playing a regular round and time is running out and they ring that bell off-screen to give the wheel a final spin to assign dollar value to the letters.

The thing I hate about this is there's always one contestant who did really well the entire show. And they worked for it! $200 a letter. $400 a letter. To build the lead they deserved!

But now, just because we're a little tight on time, vowels are worth nothing! Consonants are worth . . . $25,000 a letter!

And the one moron who didn't get anything right the entire show gets to guess first!

"Is there an H?"

TEN FUCKING H'S FLASH ON THE BOARD!

A quarter of a million dollars in 10 seconds!

"I'd like to solve the puzzle, Pat . . ."

"Go ahead. It's a phrase . . ."

"SHHHHHHHHHH"

Maybe it's time to start watching Jeopardy.

CHAPTER 19

A NIGHT TO REMEMBER

It's a cold February evening in 2015 and I'm in the green room of Magooby's Joke House in the Baltimore suburb of Timonium, waiting for Dom Irrera to arrive.

Magooby's sits in a nondescript industrial park that also houses a post office and a gun range. (Theoretically, you could bomb on stage, walk up the hill and work it off by spraying automatic weapons fire at a target for 45 minutes. It's a form of therapy I myself have not tried – yet. Plus I hear bullets are way pricier than booze.)

Magooby's is my home club now, even though I only do about a dozen gigs a year. On this night, I've been booked to open for Dom once again, and I'm both nervous and excited.

Aside from briefly bumping into him years ago at the Borgata Hotel in Atlantic City – I was there to see Brad Garrett perform and Dom was performing in another club – I haven't really seen or talked to Dom since opening for him in 2003 at the Baltimore Improv.

This is the reunion I've been waiting for since that memorable dinner with him in Little Italy after our last gig together.

In the meantime, it's been 12 years of on-and-off comedy for me. Twelve years of scrounging for material and polishing my act. Twelve years of dreams come true and 12 years of close calls and big-time disappointments in a business that can be as cold and cruel as they come.

Twelve years of my life have gone by. I'm wondering what the great Dom Irrera will think of me now.

Will he be happy that I'm still performing? Will he acknowledge that my act has grown, that I'm much more poised and funny in front of audiences now?

Will he think it's sad – even pitiable – that I'm still an opening act in the Baltimore area?

Will he even *remember* me?

Who knows, maybe to Dom, I'm just one of hundreds of young comics he's run into during his storied career, young comics who want to do what he's done, who want to achieve the success and respect that he's achieved, but haven't gotten there yet.

On the other hand, there's a part of me that knows – just *knows* – that whatever his initial impressions of me may be, they'll change once he sees me out on that stage.

I want him to see me *destroy* the crowd.

I want him to see how much stronger I've become on stage, how much more sophisticated my material is now. I want him to see how much I've grown as a comedian – and as an artist.

Sure, I'm not without my regrets as I sit there waiting for Dom to show.

Closing in on 40, I think about what could have happened if the comedy connections I nurtured the past 12 years, the big clubs I played, the headliners I worked with, were all just a few hundred miles north of here in New York.

Would I have been a star? Maybe. Who knows?

And while I know there are some wonderful people in that other world, Baltimore is my home. My family is here. My friends are here. And thank God for that.

Besides, whenever I start to linger too long on the regrets in my life, I think of the Roger Ebert quote at the beginning of this book, especially the part that says: "If at the end, we have done something to make others a little happier, and something to make ourselves a little happier, that is about the best we can do."

Yes, that's it exactly.

Take away all the bullshit, take away the fame and fortune and bragging rights and false perceptions of what success is, and you have this: I've been able to do what I've always dreamt of doing, which is to make people laugh.

In fact, here I am, sitting in the green room of a major comedy club, waiting to perform stand-up on the same bill as one of my idols. Again.

Do I wish I did it more? Sometimes. And sometimes I thank God I don't have to do it all the time. My day job – the one they tell you not to quit – has allowed me to live my life the way I wanted to and not be a prisoner of comedy.

In other words, when you do something because you *have* to, you tend not to love it as much as if you did it because you *want* to. And I'm not sure I would love performing comedy every night of the week.

There are guys like Mike Finazzo, a Baltimore-based comic, who perform just about every night of the week. Hell, sometimes he does more the one location on a weeknight. Mike is one of the hardest working (and talented) comics I know. He craves being on the stage. I don't think I could do what he does.

It's exhausting. It's draining. I'd have to go to the gym more. And we've already discussed my feelings on that . . .

Do I get envious of other comics' successes or achievements?

You bet.

The other day, for instance, I saw a Facebook post of Erik Myers, the comic who I started in the business with all those years ago at that Improv Funniest Person contest. He plays the Comedy Store in L.A. all the time and was doing voice-over work at the Henson Recording Studios in Hollywood. He's got an agent and is working full-time in the business.

Not that I begrudge Erik at all. But . . . what a cool fucking memory all that will be!

And that's when I go back to the quote from Ben Kurtzman in Barry Levinson's "Liberty Heights," also at the front of this book: "If I knew things would no longer be, I would have tried to remember better."

But I don't *dwell* in my envy. Uh-uh. Because here's the Larry Noto quote on that well-known of the Seven Deadly Sins: To envy someone for their great experiences is to fail to remember your own.

Not bad, if I do say so myself . . .

In any event, in the midst all this introspection and philosophizing in the green room, Dom Irrera finally arrives.

He's accompanied by Magooby's owner, Andrew Unger, a man who truly and passionately cares about comedy and comedians. But I can tell instantly that Dom doesn't remember me.

I start talking about things that might jog his memory: jokes he told when we first worked together at the Improv, advice he gave me back then, etc. Dom is polite, but this much is clear: the role he played in my life is dramatically different from the role I played in his life.

I'm just one of hundreds and hundreds of young comedians he's met on the road over the years. (I know, I know . . . big surprise.)

Nevertheless, it turns out to be another great weekend with Dom. Little by little, he starts to recall our previous gig together. And, unprompted by me, he brings up running into each other in Atlantic City. I also start hearing from other people at the club that Dom is saying nice things about me and my act.

After the final show Saturday night, Dom pulls me aside and says: "I'm really glad I got to see you again. You're really doing a great job."

He really seems to mean it, too. Hearing this from one of my comedy idols, from a performer who's had an enormous and enduring influence on my love for the art form, my heart soars.

A few minutes later, all the comedians on the bill drift over to the club's bar, Wit's End Saloon, to relax with a few drinks and meet audience members.

Dom is sitting at the bar for a while, talking with fans and a couple of old friends who've driven down from Philadelphia to see his act. I'm on the other side of the room, talking to people. But the next time I look Dom's way, the stool is empty and he's gone.

I run out into the hallway to try and catch him, but it's too late. Someone tells me the car service has already come and gone. Dom is headed back to his hotel.

It kills me that I didn't get to say good-bye. And I can't help wondering what will happen going forward.

Will I ever see the great Dom Irrera again?

Will it be another 12 years before our paths cross? And will I still be doing comedy? Hell, I'm not even sure I'll be performing 12 *weeks* from now. Or whether I'll *ever* perform again, now that my gigs are getting fewer and fewer.

But as I head back to the bar moments later, I can feel my spirits lifting already.

If this was my last time ever on a comedy stage, it was a helluva way to go out.

A full house, an appreciative audience and a comedy icon telling you you're doing great work – how many people *ever* get that kind of night?

EPILOGUE

Within two months of that exhilarating night at Magooby's, it seemed as if my whole life turned upside-down.

First came the sad revelation that my father, Joe Noto, was dying of throat cancer. And on an unseasonably cool afternoon in late April, Baltimore, the city I'd loved and championed for so long, exploded in riots, ignited by the death of a black man named Freddie Gray in police custody.

I was leaving my office at the National Aquarium that afternoon, headed for a meeting with my parents and our lawyer to discuss the future of my father's business, when I noticed a commotion in the building.

Men in suits were running for the elevators. They wore frightened expressions.

"Is something going on?" I asked.

"More protests about Freddie Gray," someone said. "They're urging people to leave the city."

Protests over his death had filled the streets two nights in a row. Outside the gates of Camden Yards, the hallowed baseball Taj Mahal where the Orioles played, the demonstrations had turned violent, with trash cans thrown and police cars damaged.

Now, with Freddie' Gray's funeral just hours old, students throwing rocks and bottles were massing near Mondawmin Mall, with a phalanx of police with helmets and shields eyeing the kids warily.

Within hours, the student unrest had morphed into a full-scale riot, with a mob of mostly older men looting and burning businesses and clashing with the police. Images of the chaos, in particular a CVS store being sacked and torched, would soon be flashed all over the world.

It would give Baltimore, a city with an already out-sized reputation for violence, an even bigger black eye. And if all the so-called expert commentators were to be believed, it would set the city's PR and marketing efforts back years.

I drove back to Bel Air with a heavy heart. And when I reached the lawyer's office, my spirits sank even more.

My dad was now very thin. He could no longer talk. His teeth and lips were stained with blood from the illness and the treatments he'd undergone. We got him a little whiteboard, on which he could write his thoughts, and he used it to crack jokes.

I marveled at the man's strength. He was still driving himself to work every day. But the end was near, and he was rushing to clear up his affairs, racing against the decline of his own body.

"Not enough time," he would write.

Now we were there to discuss what to do with Music Land, the music store he had built from the ground up over 50 years ago.

First order of business: after discussing his legacy, we decided to change the name of the company to Joe Noto's Music Land. We wanted everyone to know the store was his baby, and always would be.

My dad wrote the new name on the whiteboard and smiled. He was humble, but you could tell he was proud, too.

As the meeting went on, news text alerts started popping up on my phone. Then came texts from my friends: "Do you see what's happening in Baltimore?" and "Are you OK?"

Baltimore was in chaos. The looting and burning would go on all day and well into the night, leaving the city in shock and its citizens fearful of what was to come.

My dad said good-bye to his life's work at that meeting. And that night, deep in my soul, I said good-bye to my life's work, too.

My dad died a week later. He was in a great deal of pain for two days. But his last 24 hours were peaceful, a gift to him and everyone in the family, and a time of great reflection.

In the hours and days after his death, we heard from hundreds and hundreds of people who wrote and called and posted kind words on-line about what Joe Noto and the store had meant in their lives.

It was during this time that I began to think about my own future, too.

My dad's store – and his legacy – meant so much to so many people, and I didn't want to see that just fade away.

So after weeks of reflection, even as Baltimore rose from the ashes again, I made the biggest decision of my life. I resigned from my position as director of marketing at the aquarium. For the first time in 20 years, I would not be commuting to the city and back.

Instead, I'd now be running Joe Noto's Music Land.

I'd be doing something that – in a fresh and different way – would have an impact on thousands of people's lives.

And finally, I'd be controlling my own destiny.

Well, as much as any of us can.

But it's not like I plan to ever completely give up comedy. No, it's too hard-wired into my DNA, even if the day comes when I do only a few gigs a year. I still love the rush, still love the thrill of climbing on a stage and making people laugh.

Not long after taking over Joe Noto's Music Land, I was eating at a diner in Timonium when my cell phone rang. I didn't recognize the number. But I recognized the L.A. area code and answered.

It was Dom Irrera.

We didn't chat for long. He had just called to say how much he'd enjoyed working with me again at Magooby's, and how far my act had come. And he thanked me for some photos I'd taken of him and his Philly friends in the green room.

There wasn't a lot to the phone call. It didn't change my life. It didn't make me famous or get me more work as a comedian.

But now it meant more to me than any of those things ever would.

This was the good-bye from Dom I'd been looking for.

Just as he was all those years ago, Dom was still out there, still playing A-list clubs on the road and killing it. And I was still here. Living my life, remembering some amazing moments, and making people laugh whenever I could.

Not much had changed – and everything had changed.

And I was finally happy with that.

That's my time. You've been a great crowd. Enjoy the rest of the show!

I know I will . . .

ABOUT THE AUTHORS

Larry Noto is a storyteller across a multitude of media. In comedy, he's entertained audiences in major clubs in New York City, Las Vegas, Washington, D.C., California and Baltimore and opened for some of the biggest names in the business – Brad Garrett, Lewis Black, Richard Lewis, Brian Regan, Bob Saget and more. In radio and television, he's worked on-air and as a producer and even earned an Emmy nomination for his work at the ABC affiliate in Baltimore.

As an award winning marketing professional, he's held positions with Visit Baltimore, Harbor Magic Hotels in Baltimore's Inner Harbor and most recently, National Aquarium.

Noto now helps to keep the story of his father's legacy alive by running Joe Noto's Music Land, one of the largest full-service music stores in the Mid-Atlantic region. He lives in Bel Air, Maryland with five Muppets and thirteen Christmas trees.

Kevin Cowherd is the author, along with Hall of Famer Cal Ripken Jr., of *The New York Times* best-seller *Hothead* and four other baseball novels for young readers. His last book for Apprentice House Press was *Hale Storm: The Incredible Saga of Baltimore's Ed Hale, Including a Secret Life with the CIA.*

He has also written for *Men's Health, Parenting* and *Baseball Digest* magazines and is the author of a collection of columns, "Last Call at the 7-Eleven." He was an award-winning sports columnist and features writer for *The Baltimore Sun* for 32 years before leaving the newspaper in 2013.

Apprentice House is the country's only campus-based, student-staffed book publishing company. Directed by professors and industry professionals, it is a nonprofit activity of the Communication Department at Loyola University Maryland.

Using state-of-the-art technology and an experiential learning model of education, Apprentice House publishes books in untraditional ways. This dual responsibility as publishers and educators creates an unprecedented collaborative environment among faculty and students, while teaching tomorrow's editors, designers, and marketers.

Outside of class, progress on book projects is carried forth by the AH Book Publishing Club, a co-curricular campus organization supported by Loyola University Maryland's Office of Student Activities.

Eclectic and provocative, Apprentice House titles intend to entertain as well as spark dialogue on a variety of topics. Financial contributions to sustain the press's work are welcomed. Contributions are tax deductible to the fullest extent allowed by the IRS.

To learn more about Apprentice House books or to obtain submission guidelines, please visit www.apprenticehouse.com.

Apprentice House
Communication Department
Loyola University Maryland
4501 N. Charles Street
Baltimore, MD 21210
Ph: 410-617-5265 • Fax: 410-617-2198
info@apprenticehouse.com • www.apprenticehouse.com